Rescue Dog Rehoming Remedies – Volume One

Eleven Dog Training Secrets and Stories from the World's Leading Rescue Dog Trainers

Compiled by Dominic Hodgson with contributions from Katie Guastapaglia, Dan Alberts, Carol Clark, Tim Jackson, Suzanne Gould, Steven Wylie, Adam Delderfield, Emma Lee, Sarah Bartlett
and Karen Boyce

Dedication

This book is dedicated to all the amazing volunteers who keep small independent animal's rescues open and operating 24/7, 365 days a year.

You provide a sanctuary for the most desperate dogs in our society, and you make the world a better, more hopeful place.

P.S. Dear reader, please do whatever you can to support your local rescue.

Published by

Elite Publishing Academy

www.elitepublishingacademy.com

First Edition published 2020

Printed and bound in Great Britain by

www.elitepublishingacademy.com

A catalogue record for this book

is available from The British Library

ISBN

978-1-912713-24-0

Contents

Introduction

In late 2018 I had an idea to do a charity bike ride where I would visit rescue centres all over the UK

I say 'idea'. It was more of a brain fart if I'm honest.

See, I'd just finished reading (for the third time) French Revolutions by Tim Moore. In that book, Tim rides the entire route of the Tour de France. I love France (who doesn't love croissants, cakes and Rose wine?) I love the Tour de France, and I used to love cycling when I was a kid.

Also, I'd recently bought a secondhand bike, and I was desperate to enrol in a race or an event that would force me to take the cycling seriously enough, so I could actually lose a bit of tub and get fit for the first time in ten years.

I knew my wife wouldn't react too well to me following Tim's lead, and buggering off to France for three weeks, so I needed another plan.

Then, one night I was lying in bed wide awake wondering why the previous house owners had wallpapered the ceiling when the idea struck me.

It was dogs.

Specifically, rescue dogs.

My love of rescue dogs was the missing ingredient.

I should confess, I haven't always been a dog man.

I grew up in a non-dog owning family, and apart from watching Scooby doo every week, I wasn't really bothered about dogs for the first half of my life. However, dogs and rescue dogs in particular have been a constant presence in my life since I was 20 years old, when Beth, our newborn son Alex and I moved into our first council house.

Beth was at University training to be a teacher; I was a jobbing club singer, and we really didn't have a pot to piss in. So, three weeks after moving in, we probably couldn't have picked a worse time to head off to our local shelter and pick up a nine-week-old ratbag of a mongrel we called Flo.

Flo was a bitch, in every sense of the word. No doubt, my inexperience made her bad behaviour far worse. That and an over-reliance on getting dog training advice from Mexican TV stars left me feeling confused about dog ownership, and I knew I wouldn't be in line to receive dog owner of the year any time soon.

Things must have improved because six years later we welcomed Barry the 18-month-old rescue Dogue de Bordeaux into the family.

As with all rescue dogs, Barry came with some issues (you'll find out more about Barry in chapter 11) but overall, he was a truly amazing dog, a fantastic teacher, and a great ambassador for rescue dogs.

A few years later, I was getting bored with my day job as a rep selling cigarettes to corner shops, and I needed a new hobby to get me out in the fresh air. So, I decided to give something back to the rescues who had given us two amazing pets, and I started volunteering at my local shelter. I'd spend a couple of afternoons a week walking the dogs that were waiting rehoming.

That experience inspired me to start my own dog adventure business in 2011, and two years later, I started on the path to becoming a dog trainer when I attended a John Rogerson 7-day dog behaviour course. I had an amazing mentor in local dog training legend David Davies, who helped me perfect my 'play' philosophy. In 2015 I wrote my first dog training book *How to Be Your Dog's Superhero,* which featured all of the mistakes I'd made with Barry and Flo.

Since then, my simple dog training mission has been to help dogs and owners enjoy fantastic, fun, stress-free relationships together. I think if an owner knows how to make their dog happy, and the dog gets all of his enjoyment in life from his owner, then dog ownership becomes a lot easier, and fewer dogs end up in rescue.

So, I knew if I could put together an event that would combine my love of cycling, rescue dogs, and would bring together all the amazing pet professionals I've met in the last decade, then I would be onto something pretty special.

At the very least I'd raise some cash for local rescues and get a few days away exploring the UK on my bike. And so, the Tour de Rescue was born.

The event took place over four days in early September 2019. I roped in my good friend Alex 'The video guy' Wardle, to film the whole thing. He brought along his partner Nomsi to assist him, and my dad also came along as a one-man support team.

Despite a few hiccups (and wrong turns), the event went off without too much drama, and over four days I cycled 180 miles as we visited 15 rescues in Northumberland, Teeside, the Peak District and North Wales.

The 'tour' ticked many boxes for me but the main one was to highlight the amazing dogs that are available in rescue centres, and the great work done by rescue centre volunteers all over the UK.

I wanted to give the small local rescues a chance to tell their story, *and* the inspirational stories of the dogs in their care, to try and take away the stigma that rescue dogs have of being 'damaged goods'.

They aren't.

Yes, rescue dogs need help, love, guidance from understanding and patient owners, but then so do puppies and any other kind of dog.

Most of the dogs I saw in the rescue centres would make amazing pets for owners who are prepared to put some time and effort into providing the dogs with a consistent routine, which gives them an outlet for all their doggy needs.

There are a lot of things we can do to reduce the number of dogs in rescue, and I don't think the answer lies in simply building more and rescue centres.

Getting rid of all puppy farms and introducing dog-owning licenses are just two of the suggestions I heard on my travels. I think both have merit.

I wanted the Tour de Rescue to have a lasting legacy, and help educate rescue dog owners or those just thinking about adopting a rescue dog. So, in three of the four locations the tour visited, we did an evening of 'Rescue dog' themed seminars. I also got a bunch of my dog training friends to contribute dog training articles to the Tourderescue.com website.

And, as the Corona-crisis has put the kibosh on me doing another Tour this year, I decided to take this a step further and create a permanent 'Rescue Dog Recourse' in the form of a book filled with actionable, practical, useful and inspirational rescue dog training stories and advice.

This is the book you are holding in your hands now.

Upfront, I'd like to express my sincere thanks to all the amazing contributors to the Rescue Dog Rehoming Remedies; dog trainers and writers Katie Guastapaglia, Dan Alberts, Carol Clark, Tim Jackson, Suzanne Gould, Steven Wylie, Adam Delderfield, Emma Lee, Sarah Bartlett and Karen Boyce. Thanks also to Ben Waters who donated the Tour de Rescue website and to Julia Brown who designed and donated the Tour de Rescue logo.

Rescue dogs ask so little yet add so much to our lives.

I genuinely wouldn't be doing what I am now if it wasn't for rescue dogs.

I hope this book helps you better understand your rescue dog and enables you to enjoy a better life together.

Enjoy!

Dom Hodgson

Katie Guastapaglia

At the Other Side of Every Fear Is Freedom

We set off from Tuscany at 6 o'clock in the morning, reaching Milan around ten. The whole journey I kept checking the photo on my phone as the landscape became flatter and the hills receded into the distance.

'I wonder what he'll do when he sees us!'

'I *can't wait* to meet him!'

The handsome orange and white Bracco, I checked his headshot one more time. I was like a child at Christmas.

The sat-nav told us we had arrived. We pulled off down a long, narrow country road and into the rescue centre.

Growing up we always adopted our dogs from Dogs Trust Darlington, and I used to love going along to see the dogs and took food and bedding for them. Dogs Trust Harefield, the rehoming centre closest to Dogs Trust's London Head Office where I later worked was a newer, even slicker version of the yellow and black haven I'd grown to love. Fifi, who was currently being cared for by a neighbour while we made the eight-hour round trip to Milan, was adopted from Battersea Dogs and Cats Home. Dogs Trust and Battersea: The Hiltons of the rescue world.

The rescue centre in Milan was not The Hilton. It wasn't even a Travelodge.

It was a great big field, and in it running wild was a pack of around twenty dogs. I couldn't even tell which one he was.

It took ages for the kennel staff to separate him from the others and get him on a lead. He was skin and bone, and he wouldn't look at us.

I'm not criticizing the rescue centre. Like many small organisations, they were doing the best they could with what they had, and it *was*, of course, The Hilton compared to where he'd come from.

It had just been his third birthday the microchip told us. Ruben went off to complete the adoption forms with the kennel staff, leaving me alone with Lao.

I held his lead and gingerly tossed a few pieces of hotdog his way. There was a weird creeping disturbed feeling in my stomach; this dog was not alright. I gently lifted his lips.

Stumps level with the gum line and a mouth full of broken teeth.

'*Certo ha tre anni?*' I cautiously asked when the kennel staff returned. 'Are you sure he's three years old? He looks different from the photo.'

All the way home he wouldn't look at us. We didn't look at him either, not wanting to put any pressure on him. Reuben and I spoke very little, we didn't really know what to say.

Traffic piled up on the autostrada, there'd been an accident, and we lost two hours. The bright Milanese day turned into grey skies, thunder and driving rain as the car climbed back up to the gloomy mountains. We met our neighbour in the arranged neutral place, all of us soaked to the skin, to introduce the new dog to Fifi.

The introduction had been planned in minute detail. We would meet the neighbour and Fifi, spend some time doing a scent introduction and then parallel walking so they could get to know each other. It was dark, and we were drenched, Fifi took one look at Lao and dismissed him as not worth the effort. She stood there and shivered at us in disdain.

Back at the house, Fifi went straight to her bed beside the radiator. Lao stood in the kitchen and stared at the floor. I tried to encourage him over to show him the new bed we'd bought for him. He wasn't budging, so I brought it into the kitchen. He was clearly scared of us; we left him in peace.

That night I lay awake wondering what we had done, the realisation sinking in that our lives had quickly and dramatically changed and there was no going back. At that point, I couldn't know just how right I was.

The next morning I came downstairs and found him curled up in the big old brick fireplace in the kitchen. My heart broke for him. Sheltered on five sides, it was the place he felt safest.

We took him to the garden on lead to toilet, and while he was outside, we moved his bed into the fireplace. I rang my vet in the UK. He still didn't look at us.

There he stayed for two weeks: shut down and living in a fireplace. I wondered if he wanted to die.

But no. He ate! Wow, did he have an appetite!

It gave us hope. Seeing how much he loved food made us realise that he hadn't given up, so neither would we. The turning point came when Reuben came home from Pisa one day towards the end of the second week. Lao got up from the fireplace and came to greet him at the door – wagging his tail for the first time. It was a moment I'll never forget.

Lao was handed over to the rescue centre by a vet who refused to put him to sleep. He had been brought in by his ex-owners, a hunting kennel in Southern Italy because he didn't hunt well. As Lao's physical health started to improve, and we started going for walks, I began to understand that he had training and behavioural issues that wouldn't be so easily fixed. Although he'd clearly had an awful time with the hunters, his natural desire to chase prey was still strong, and I was struggling to find a safe outlet for his predatory instincts.

He would also bark and lunge at people and dogs to scare them away, even biting them. He chased rabbits, birds, anything that moved. We kept him on lead, and our daily walks became less stressful at least – but they were also boring. Lao seemed unfulfilled and frustrated. I felt guilty.

Back in the UK, I started seeking out weird and wonderful places where he could be free to run, sniff and play. Several times I thought I'd found the perfect place… then I'd turn up one morning to find that someone had got there first. My search became more extreme, the places more isolated. I didn't always feel safe.

Yet I risked it. Every time. Because I hated the idea of this energetic dog who loved running free being constantly restrained.

'If we can just get through this one walk without seeing a dog…' you know the script.

He was affecting my safety, quality of life and even my relationships as my obsession for finding off-lead spaces became evermore extreme and ridiculous.

I was at my wit's end. Something had to change.

How could I help this funny, sweet and affectionate but incredibly fearful dog live a fulfilled life? There seemed to be just one solution.

'***I need to buy a field for Lao.***'

If my friends and family didn't think I was mad already, they did now. If I said I wanted to open a private hire dog exercise field, they probably would have understood more. But we didn't buy the field to start a business; its purpose was to solve a huge problem in my life.

The first time I unclipped Lao's lead in the field that would eventually become Dogwood West, I knew that our lives had changed for the better.

He didn't stop running – he explored every centimetre of hedgerow – he sniffed every particle of scent from the long grass. With regular visits to the field, I watched his confidence grow.

I spent a wonderful, peaceful and truly life-changing first summer in that field. We took picnics, splashed about in paddling pools, played on the logs, tyres and Adventure Play frames.

We practised the sports we already knew – scentwork and parkour – and created ones of our own. I invented little courses, new positions and challenges, made up names for them. We practised every day and got really good at it. I watched Lao's confidence grow even further as he realised what he was capable of and that the world wasn't such a scary place after all. We started doing it at home too, out on our regular walks. I gave it a name: *Scentventure.*

The Four Cornerstones of Scentventure

Scentventure started with Lao and me just pottering around in a field, but it grew into something hugely beneficial for him. I suggest you use this framework for playing and interacting with your own rescue dog too. It will help you bond with them, and it will certainly make walking and exercising them much easier.

The four key cornerstones of Scentventure;

- Scentwork – for calm, focus and confidence
- Environment – for physical wellbeing
- Exploration – for mental wellbeing
- Partnership – for trust, bond, relationship and focus

Cornerstone 1: Scentwork

Sniffing, searching, scenting and finding is naturally rewarding for all dogs, but rescue dogs may especially benefit. Nervous dogs increase in confidence and anxious or overly excited dogs become calm and focused. Dogs that are normally highly distracted by the environment learn to search with no loss of focus on the task in hand.

Cornerstone 2: Environment

Obstacles in your home, garden or walks are repurposed for adventure. Work on balance, coordination, strength and endurance. The result is calm confidence and a feeling of safety.

Cornerstone 3: Exploration

Dogs are naturally curious. Humans tend to dislike this curiosity and train our dogs to be more passive. Providing new smells, new sounds, new tastes, new textures and new environments for your dog to explore taps into their natural doggy instincts and makes them calmer and happier.

Cornerstone 4: Partnership

Spending time together and working as a team builds trust, confidence, love and creates a feeling of safety, which are essential to strengthening the bond you have with your rescue dog. This improved relationship creates a dog that's more focused on you and ignores the many distractions out there.

Now I help other rescue dogs and their owners connect with Scentventure as Lao did. Reactive dogs, easily distracted dogs, bored dogs, dogs that need something to keep them out of trouble can all excel at it. The four cornerstones are always present on my in-person and online Scentventure courses.

Freedom

Although Lao's transformation may never be complete, our lives have been transformed for the better. He is happy to meet new people, walk past dogs without reacting, and we enjoy Scentventure together every day. He is a visibly happier dog, and I am a more relaxed human. The twice-daily dread of the impending walk, the excuses and apologies, the after-hours walks and bizarre locations are a thing of the past. What Lao and I have achieved most dog owners take for granted, but to us, we have moved worlds.

It was a warm evening after closing time, the birds were twittering as they settled for the night, the sun setting over Bishopton, purple orange and gold. I stood watching Lao roll around on his back, his comical long ears flew, his legs kicked in the air. His body and mind were free.

If we'd had a safe space to let Lao off when we first adopted him, to bond with him and test his recall, we could have avoided the bites, the disappearing acts, the trauma.

I want you and your rescue dog to experience the same fear-free, off-lead experience as Lao and I have at Dogwood Adventure Play, the North East's first dog adventure park.

Your rescue dog was born to run and play, and at Dogwood you can give them what they need whilst you can enjoy a relaxing, stress-free adventure walk with your best friend.

About the Author

Katie 'Queen of the Fields' Guastapaglia

Dog Trainer and Canine Enrichment Specialist, Katie runs Dogwood Adventure Play, the North East's first adventure playground for dogs. In her previous role as Campaigns Officer at Dogs Trust, she travelled across the North of England offering training, behaviour, enrichment, health and legal advice to hundreds of dog owners every week and developing new campaigns for responsible dog ownership.

A strong advocate of rescue dogs, Katie volunteered at Battersea Dogs Home before joining the Dogs Trust Head Office team where she helped deliver the campaign to parliament for compulsory microchipping.

Katie works hard to improve the lives of the dogs she works with and believes that reward-based training and enrichment are key to a strong and long-lasting relationship.

www.dogwoodadventureplay.com

Can You Teach an Old Dog New Tricks?

How I helped Gus make the move from the Spanish mountains to the City streets of Newcastle.

A few years ago, I travelled to Spain to work alongside world-famous dog trainer Nando Brown in his boarding kennels.

The kennels are out in the wilds of willy. A 45 minute drive from the nearest English speaking place and a 20 minute drive from the nearest Spanish speaking village, we really were in the arse end of nowhere.

There was no one around. Me, Nando and two others. Occasionally the local goat herder would pop by but apart from that we were alone.

Anyway, after working for a few days, I started to get to know the dogs, and one stood out from all of the rest. Old Man Gus.

Gus was a one-off. All of the dogs would go into the exercise area to go to the toilet, have a play around and a cuddle. Gus went to the toilet and then straight to the gate so that he could get back to his bed. Bed is Gus's favourite thing in the world.

I'd really taken a liking to Gus and decided to ask about him. I knew he was a permanent resident at the kennels, and I liked the idea of adopting him as my own if I moved to Spain permanently.

It turns out that Gus had been a stray. For the full nine and a half years of his life he had wandered the mountains of Almogia, eating from the bins and avoiding humans.

Now it's important to understand that in the Spanish mountains they are really bloody old school. Dogs are nothing but a farming implement or a nuisance to the locals. Strays would steal food and tear up crops. If a local got close enough, they would give them a damn good beating.

Needless to say, the strays avoid humans like we have the plague. Gus was no different.

Nando often saw Gus hovering around the communal bins and tried to make friends with him. Gus would simply turn his back and run away. Fight or flight. Safety first.

Months later (and only a couple of months before I turned up at the kennels) Gus walked to the top of the mountain, a twenty-five minute walk up very steep slopes, sat down in front of the gates and waited.

Nando noticed him, came out, tried to speak to him and Gus… stayed exactly where he was. He'd been attacked by another dog and was in a VERY bad way.

His head had become so infected that his neck and head had swelled into one large ball with a tiny point on top that was the tip of his massive ear.

Gus clearly knew he was at death's door because he stood completely still as Nando slipped a lead on, picked him up and drove him to the vets. He was in so much pain that even under a load of strong anaesthetic, he still cried, twitched and moved whilst unconscious.

After having the bite wounds cleaned and stitched, the infection treated with antibiotics and his balls chopped off they thought he was in the clear.

He was taken back to the kennels, given a nice comfy bed with blankets in his own space and was brought food twice a day, every day. Gus must have thought he had died and gone to heaven.

But he wasn't out of the woods yet. He had an allergic reaction to his castration (who wouldn't), and his empty ball sack swelled to the size of a small melon. Not only that, but it became clear that he had an infection inside his nose.

Long story short he went in for another operation and had to go through extensive treatment for his nose infection which has left the inside of it a total mess. One small tap and it begins to drip blood, and it didn't stop for days.

Anyway, by the time I got to the kennels, Gus was back to full fitness. He was enjoying his retirement, sleeping on a comfy bed, being given food twice a day and knew he was safe for the first time in his life.

The only problem for Gus was that he was going to have to spend the rest of his life at the kennels because nobody wanted him.

I mean, if you think about it, why would you want an old dog like Gus? You're just asking for a shit storm of problems.

A dog that had spent almost ten years wandering the mountains on his own, never having worn a lead, being scared of humans his whole life, scavenging and possibly killing to feed himself. And that's not to mention the health problems he had faced. Nor the fact that he was almost ten years old.

Well, you can guess what happened next. I fell in love with the bloke, then I left Spain and came back to sunny Newcastle.

Gus had two potential homes fall through for him. No one wanted him.

When I found out that someone was planning on taking him to their home in South Africa, I felt strangely disappointed. I wanted that big man in my life, and so when that fell through I moved quickly.

Two months later Gus left the warm, quiet, peaceful tranquillity of the Spanish mountains behind and made his way north to the rainy, cloudy, noisy, shit storm that is Newcastle.

And that's when I realised how much work I was going to have to do with him.

See Gus's reaction to everything he didn't know was to bark at it. That doesn't seem so bad at first until you realise that he didn't know ANYTHING.

The wind whistling through our windows, kids, cars, horse's hooves on tarmac, fireworks, slamming doors, the sound of the telly… you name it, Gus barked at it.

He had no idea how to walk on a lead and wanted to get to every dog, kid or person that he saw either through the window or on the walk (and god knows what he would do if he did get to them).

Luckily, I had been expecting a lot of these things and had prepared for them, but I was still stung by some of the things I hadn't thought of. See I have another dog, a little terrier cross called Titch, and she is absolutely perfect. I had forgotten about some of the problems dog owners face like chewing, weeing and pooing indoors, tearing apart the bin (quite a stupid one to forget considering the big man had spent his life scavenging for food) and people knocking at the door.

Needless to say, I had my work cut out.

But this brings me to the question I asked at the beginning of this.

Can you teach an old dog new tricks?

Well let me tell you, if you believe you can't, then come and spend a bit of time with Gus.

Two years later and he was absolutely perfect. He lazed around the place, eating his food, demanding cuddles from anyone and everyone. He no longer reacts to people or dogs. He's no longer scared. All Gus wants is cuddles, food and a nice soft bed to curl up in.

So yes, you certainly can teach old dogs new tricks, and funnily enough, these "tricks" are the same tricks that every dog owner should teach their dog.

Now, I don't mean tricks as in "roll-over", "play-dead", or "do a summersault on a skateboard".

No, I mean that there are tricks that owners can use every day with their dogs that will help their manners improve, help them know exactly what you want from them and will help you have a relaxed, happy and fun life with your dog.

I have taught all of my training clients about these tricks, and it has changed the lives they lead with their dogs.

I used these tricks with Little Titch when I first got her as a puppy, and I couldn't ask for a better dog.

I used these tricks with Old Man Gus when he arrived in Newcastle. He couldn't be happier in his new home, and I couldn't be happier with him.

For now, I'll tell you about the thing I had to spend the most time working on with Gus - reactivity.

Reactivity comes in all shapes and sizes, and, to a greater or lesser degree, almost every dog faces some reactivity issues in their lives.

For Titch, it's having dogs harass her.

For Gus… well when we first got Gus he was reactive to almost everything.

But before we get started let me kick the big, fat, hairy elephant out of the room.

You might know that Gus suffered from quite a big stroke and was really struggling. We tried our best to help him through, to give him time to adjust, to get used to his new life and to give him every chance that we possibly could to improve.

In the end, it didn't work.

My wife, Lyneisha, and I had to make the decision to let Gus go.

He had become deaf and blind on his left side. He was almost constantly stressed. He lost all of the strength in his back legs. He couldn't go for walks. He had to be carried up and down the stairs (especially difficult when you live in an upstairs flat and when Gus weighed almost as much as my wife).

In the end, nothing was improving, most things were getting worse, and it got to the stage where I could see in Gus's eye's that he wasn't happy and that he was in pain.

So, we had to let him go, which is why writing about this is very difficult for me.

You see, reactivity is a thing that I have A LOT of experience in thanks to Gus, and I know reactivity is something a lot of rescue dog owners have to live with.

I have contemplated teaching this handy little exercise in a totally different way so that I didn't have to sit and think about my Big Man, but I have decided that a few tears from a trip down memory lane will be worth it if Gus's story can help you a little bit.

So here we go…

When I was working in the Spanish kennels, and Gus was a resident, you always knew that Gus was there.

How? Because his default reaction to anything and everything was to bark.

Someone entered the kennels, and Gus barked.

Someone walked past his kennel, and he barked.

When it got close to meal time, he barked.

No matter what happened, Gus barked.

In fact, I even remember waking up one night in the pitch black, in the early hours of the morning, and I could hear Gus barking.

It was a nightmare.

And so, when Lyneisha and I sat down to talk about bringing him over here, I knew that we would have to do something about the barking.

Barking at everything and anything might be acceptable in the lonely Spanish mountains, but it is not acceptable to bark at everything and anything in the middle of Newcastle.

That sort of thing is known as reactivity and, theoretically, could lead to him getting killed and his owner, me, getting a criminal record.

Not cool.

Lyneisha and I had to decide what we were going to do about this because it was a lot of risk.

Our lives were pretty perfect at the time.

Home was our sanctuary.

It was calm. It was easy. It was quiet. It was exactly how we wanted it to be.

Gus could turn that on its head.

To our knowledge he had never met children before, he had never seen large cars, motorways (we live close to one), horses, shops (we live above one), deliveries to the shops in the early hours of the morning, fireworks, studded boots, laminate flooring, carpet…

You name it, Gus had never seen it before, and I was willing to bet quite a lot of money that his first reaction to all of those things would be to bark at it.

Needless to say, I was right about the barking.

He barked at everything and everyone, all day long.

It was a nightmare.

There were times when I wanted to pick him, put him on a plane and send him back to those Spanish mountains.

That boy could bark! And he barked loud!

Quite a big difference from tiny little Titch who never made a sound and was never a pick of bother.

But luckily, we knew he was going to be reactive to everything, and so we had planned.

I had done my research, and I had asked for advice from a few different people.

Forgive me for a second as I get all technical and scientific.

Basically, I decided to use a desensitisation and counter-conditioning protocol to turn Gus from a Barking Bloody Brute to a Silent Smiley Shepherd.

Now, let's not all get too excited by the big words.

Let me try that again in real person speak.

I decided to show Gus that everything wasn't scary by slowly exposing him to new things over time, whilst helping him realise that everything that could be scary is actually going to be a really good thing for him.

I wanted him to see anything he wasn't sure about as a potentially exciting thing for him.

I wanted to show him that if there was ever anything he was unsure about, checking in with me would turn that thing into an exciting thing for him.

So, the second Gus walked through my door I set to work and here's what I did.

Firstly, I needed him to understand when he had done something right and when he was going to get a reward.

I used what is known as a "marker" for that. You basically mark a behaviour that you like by using a word or a clicker.

From day one, I started to get Gus used to the sound of a clicker and the word "Yes!". I wanted him to know that whatever he had just done was going to get him a reward.

Now as you will know, a clicker isn't always necessary.

A marker word like "Yes!" can and does work just as effectively. Plus you have the added bonus of still being able to reward your dog if you forget your clicker.

But I wanted to use a clicker for two very important reasons:

Speed and Precision.

I don't know about you, but I can click a clicker a lot quicker than I can say yes.

Also, saying yes is a much longer process, and as a result, it is not as precise.

I needed to be able to mark Gus's behaviour immediately before he started barking and so a clicker would work perfectly.

Let me explain why.

When your dog is about to react to something, his body posture will change.

His ears will perk up.

His body will go rigid.

He will most likely turn and face whatever direction the distraction is coming from.

The body posture is our first indicator that our dog has heard or seen something and that he is getting ready to react to it.

Luckily, I could cheat with Gus.

His ears were so bloody big that I couldn't miss it when he heard something.

Anyway, my plan was this.

As soon as Gus heard something, I needed to mark his behaviour BEFORE he had the chance to bark.

So when he heard a firework, I would click as soon as I heard the firework and I would make a big, noisy fuss of him to distract him from the noise, get him excited and make it all as rewarding as possible.

Because it was so rewarding for him I knew he would come to me, he'd get a bit of food and a cuddle, and then he would settle again.

When he went to the toilet in our back yard, I would stand in the doorway and watch him.

As soon as he would hear a noise… "Click" or "Yes!"…before he had the chance to bark.

I wanted to reward him for hearing or seeing the distraction and not reacting to it.

But because I knew he was going to react to almost everything I really had to be on the ball.

I had to be quick. I had to click as soon as he heard it and make a big enough fuss to distract him from it.

Eventually, things started to turn around, and he totally got it. For example, on his first Bonfire night, I closed the windows and curtains, I put the television on loud, and I sat in the living room with a huge bowl of cheese and chicken.

When the first fireworks went off, I clicked, and I treated. I made a big fuss. He got chicken. He got cheese. He got cuddles. And then I would let him go and do his thing.

When the next firework went off, we did the same thing all over again.

Before the end of the fireworks display, he started looking around, waiting for the fireworks to go off. When they did, he would spin around and come right at me, ready to get his cheese, chicken and cuddles.

And he did that without barking.

It was amazing.

I cannot tell you how happy I was. How proud I was.

Gus really was a special dog.

He achieved so much in so little time with us.

He went from a stressed-out dog who reacted to everything, barking at it to keep it away, to being a lazy old man who loved nothing more than to lie in his bed and let life and all of its noises, distractions and issues go on around him whilst he slept.

I can honestly say that I cannot remember the last time I heard Gus bark before he died.

Nothing fazed him.

He ignored other dogs that annoyed him by just turning away from them.

He looked at me when loud noises scared and shocked him.

He looked at me whenever he was in a situation that he was unsure about.

He no longer needed to protect himself because he trusted that I would never let anything happen to him.

And I like to think I did always protect him.

Right up until his last day.

I hope you find this helpful. This exercise changed everything for us, and I hope it can do the same for you.

RIP Gus mate.

About the Author

Dan Alberts

Dan Alberts is a dog trainer from Newcastle who wants to help you build your relationship with your dog by becoming his best friend. Dan believes that by being your Dog's Best Friend and having a Perfect Recall you and your dog can have the stress-free and fulfilled life that you always dreamed of.

How to change your rescue dog's unwanted behaviour?

Clare was fed up with Max. He just wouldn't listen to her at all. She almost wished she hadn't been taken in by those big puppy eyes at the rescue centre three weeks ago.

She knew he was still just a puppy at six months old, but his charging round the house, stealing and chewing toys, socks and shoes, jumping up at the children when they were playing in the garden, begging for (and stealing) food, and tripping her up by getting under her feet all the time, was getting her down.

She was trying to train him, but the things she read in books weren't helping her change how Max behaved.

She was really struggling.

If you've recently adopted a rescue puppy, you're probably feeling the same as Clare. I certainly was when I brought home my rescue dog, Mack. He hardly slept and was a manic nightmare round the house.

It's really tiring dealing with a new dog of any age, but especially a nearly fully grown puppy who hasn't learnt any manners.

Just when you think you've sorted the house-training and stopped the nipping and biting, your sweet, cute little bundle of fluff morphs into a gangly, obnoxious teenager.

His puppy behaviours aren't so funny anymore. They're annoying, frustrating - and sometimes expensive.

It's all too easy to ignore your rescue dog's bad behaviour because you feel sorry for him.

We all have tough times, and it's easy to wallow in a vat of self-pity, but pacing around with a hand on your fevered brow saying "woe is me, I should never have got a rescue dog," or simply ignoring the problem, crossing your fingers and hoping it will improve of its own accord, is pointless.

The bad news first - there are no magic bullets. If you're honest, you probably just want someone to wave a magic wand and make all of your problems go away. I often want that. But it only happens in fairy tales.

Forget that idea.

The good news is that nearly all unwanted behaviours can be stopped, changed, or improved significantly, even in a rescue dog with ingrained bad habits.

But it takes work - sometimes a LOT of work. If you're not prepared to put the work in, then you might as well stop reading now. This chapter won't help you. But please note that if you do nothing, the behaviour will almost certainly get worse – behaviours rarely stay the same. So, you need to change something.

The key principle is to make slow and steady changes to your rescue dog's routine. TO change any behaviour you have to change habits – and that takes a long time.

Sometimes habits can be even sneakier and set themselves up without us realising.

When you're eating a biscuit, your rescue dog comes up and sits in front of you, gazing at you with those pleading doggy eyes. You give him a piece, telling yourself you're rewarding his attention on you - but you're actually setting up a begging habit.

When your rescue dog steals your slipper, and you yell at him and run after him to get it back, he'll enjoy the chase game - and you're setting up a stealing habit.

When your rescue dog lunges forward on lead you stop, call him back and give him a treat beside you. But he doesn't learn to stop pulling, and you don't know why. Surely you're teaching him to be at your side by giving him a treat there? Well, no - you've set up a habit. Your dog has learnt to pull, then wait for you to call before coming back for a treat.

If your rescue dog is doing something you don't want him to do, then something has to change.

It's YOU that needs to make that change - your dog's quite happy with the status quo. He's come into your life with a load of habits that worked for him before, so why should he change things?

And you need to make the changes you want before these habit behaviours become embedded in his new forever home.

Why does my dog do what he does?

Dogs do the things that either make them feel good or help them avoid something that makes them feel uncomfortable. Behaviours are only unwanted when we deem them to be.

If something makes your dog feel good, we call that thing a reward. A reward can be all sorts of things - comfort (lying on the settee), the act of chewing (anything - including your best shoes), yummy food to eat (especially when stolen), attention from us (particularly when we're busy with something else), or satisfying a chase instinct (especially when the something chased is alive).

Your rescue dog will crave your attention. Stealing socks and shoes gets your attention and gives your dog his reward as you chase him to try and retrieve the item. Even telling your rescue dog off can be a reward - from the attention you're giving him. Or perhaps your dog's reward is the endorphin release he gets from running around after your children, or from jumping up at guests.

What behaviour does your rescue dog show to get your attention?

Here's another important point: Whether or not something is a reward depends on how your dog perceives it, not your view of it.

You may think your patting his head is rewarding - but he may dislike that type of touch. You may think giving him a piece of kibble is a reward - but your dog may not be hungry. You may think offering him his tug toy is a reward - but he may prefer to go and sniff the lamp post over there.

Here's the thing. If your rescue dog is performing a particular behaviour, then he is somehow getting a reward for doing it.

Working out what the precise reward is for your particular dog in that distinct situation is key to understanding why your dog does the behaviour - and essential when finding ways to change unwanted behaviours in any dog, not just rescue dogs.

Should I use force to make him do what I want?

Clare may be told, or read about, forceful methods to try and change Max's behaviour - to punish Max when he does something Clare doesn't want. Most people have heard of, read, or seen this sort of advice – make sure your rescue dog knows who's boss; tap your dog on the nose when he barks; hit him with a rolled-up newspaper when he toilets in the house; or squirt him with water if he's naughty.

You'll hear these sorts of things from lots of people - it sounds like normal, good advice.

Beware.

There are six big problems with using forceful techniques:

1. Punishment's an easy option for humans. It requires less brainpower to react to your dog's unwanted behaviour than to think about why your dog is doing it and how you could proactively prevent him doing it instead. It's the lazy option.
2. You need to be sure what you do is punishing to your dog. A squirt of water may indeed be unpleasant for some dogs, but others will love it, and it's a reward for them.
3. Punishment may reduce the behaviour, but only temporarily. Especially when it's not linked with rewarding acceptable behaviour.
4. It might tell your rescue dog what he shouldn't be doing, but it gives him no help at all to teach him what he should do instead.

5. Punishment will definitely harm your relationship with your rescue dog.
6. Finally, effective punishment has to be used consistently and timed perfectly. Most of us can't manage that.

Punishment just doesn't work. There are much better options.

If you punish your rescue dog for toileting on your rug, he might decide to hide his eliminations behind the curtain or sofa instead.

If you punish your dog for raiding your bin, he'll just make sure you're not around next time he wants to do it.

If you punish your rescue dog for not coming back immediately when you call, he'll be even less likely to come in future.

Your dog is not looking guilty when you come home to find your new Jimmy Choos destroyed, or a mess on the carpet. Dogs will "look guilty" if scolded or when you are cross, whether they've done something or not. The main reason for your dog "looking guilty" when you return is *your* behaviour, not anything your dog has or hasn't done. In other words, your behaviour as an owner and your history of scolding or reprimands is what makes your dog "look guilty".

If punishment doesn't work, what can I do?

First, identify what reward(s), or benefit(s), your dog is getting when they do the behaviour. The reward may be from you, or it may be from the situation or the environment.

Does he get your attention by barking?

Does she get you to move faster if she pulls on the lead?

Does he get a fuss from you when he pushes at your hand?

Do other dogs keep away when she barks at them?

Does he get food when he begs?

Does she get to eat the food she steals from the kitchen counter?

My assistants were laughing at me recently. I'd subconsciously been trained by my current dog, Gus. I was feeding him random bits of food for staying quietly by my side while I was teaching a class. He started putting his foot on top of mine, and when he did, I fed him. He'd trained me to give him food whenever he wanted, by putting his foot on mine. He'd set his own reward criteria.

Work out what reward your dog is getting.

Once you've identified the reward(s) your dog is getting for the unwanted behaviour, you need a plan.

Your plan can be cunning as a fox or may just involve a simple change in routine. It's vital to set up an acceptable new routine for your rescue dog as soon as possible after he comes home with you. It'll help him settle in more easily, and it'll set expectations he will strive to meet. Remember, your rescue dog usually just wants your attention and fuss – so set up a system to give that attention and fuss for the things you want him to do.

To change your dog's unwanted behaviour, you have two options:

OPTION 1 : Teach your dog to do something else instead (for which he gets at least an equivalent reward)

Doing something else instead can be teaching your rescue dog to go to bed instead of begging for food at the dinner table. Or to lie quietly at your side when you're working in the kitchen to avoid tripping you up. Or to lie on the grass gnawing a bone instead of destroying the garden. Or to go into his crate to eat a yummy Kong instead of jumping at the children when they're playing.

OPTION 2 : Stop the reward(s) your dog is getting for the behaviour.

Stopping the rewards can include removing the kitchen bin to stop bin raiding. Or putting food away to stop your rescue dog stealing it from the kitchen counter. Or, in my case, not giving a treat when Gus puts his paw on my foot.

Simple, yes? Yes - and no.

Dog training is indeed simple - but it's not necessarily easy. Think of that old saying: How do you eat an elephant? The answer: in bite-sized chunks. To achieve anything in life, you need to focus on the small steps and break all the big stuff down into smaller, achievable pieces.

Here's my basic three-step plan for changing your rescue dogs unwanted behaviour:

STEP 1: Decide which of the two options above you're going to use for each unwanted behaviour. With Max, Clare could teach him to "leave" to stop him stealing shoes and socks, and she could teach him "stay" to keep him from getting under her feet (option 1). Or she could use baby gates or other barriers to stop him charging round the house, and she could shut him in when the children were running around the garden (option 2).

Keep your plan as simple as possible.

STEP 2: Put your plan into action, one thing at a time. Don't try to do everything at once. Pick the unwanted behaviour you like least to address first. Or pick the one that seems easiest to do—your choice.

Use a reward your rescue dog loves to teach him what you want him to do instead. Clare decided to give Max a filled Kong in the utility room while the children were out playing. Simple and effective. Once you've dealt with that problem, move on to the next bit of your plan and do that one. One thing at a time. Keep it simple.

STEP 3: Make sure everyone in the family knows what the plan is and agrees to help, so everyone does the same thing. Consistency is key. It's no good deciding you don't want your new rescue dog up on the furniture if the children encourage him up there for a cuddle each evening. It's no good Claire trying to teach Max to settle on his bed at dinner time if her husband surreptitiously feeds him under the table.

Tell your family and friends what you want to do. Engage their help. Write it down. Put key messages up on the fridge so everyone sees them regularly.

Keep it clear and simple, and your rescue dog will soon become the perfect pet you dreamt about.

Summary

- Behaviour never stays the same - your dog will get better at it with practice. If you don't change something the behaviour will get worse
- There are two ways to change an unwanted behaviour: either teach your dog to do something else instead, or stop your dog getting the reward for it
- You need a simple, achievable, 3-step action plan that everyone will follow

About the Author

Carol Clark

As a child, Carol only wanted two things in life – to be a doctor and to have a dog. She finally achieved both aims in early adulthood. She worked hard as a doctor but seven reorganisations in eleven years took its toll, and she took early retirement.

Getting a dog with various issues and problems made her realise how little she actually knew and resulted in the years of work and study that have made her a top accredited trainer and behaviourist today. She became The Doggy Doctor and set up Down Dog Training and Behaviour in 2008. She's passionate about helping people with their problem dogs.

But she's not just about dogs. She actually set up her dog business to help fund her craft and book addictions. She enjoys a range of crafts for relaxation, including card-making, bobbin lace and crocheting rugs and toys. She's an avid reader and has far too many books clogging her shelves. And that doesn't include the thousands of books on her Kindle account…

Carol's books

Carol's has written four books, *Pesky Puppy to Perfect Pet, Chaos to Calmish, Problem Pooch Book 1: Troublesome to Tranquil, and Help! How to Socialise Your Puppy During Lockdown* are all available from Amazon as Kindle or paperback.

Find out more about the Doggy Doctor at www.downdog.co.uk

Help! My rescue dog doesn't like other dogs!

In 2010 I found out I was going to be a Daddy. This news came as a big shock as I was only 24 and was enjoying the party life as most 24 years do, but being a Daddy was something I had always wanted to be… mostly because I'm a big kid myself.

Naturally, this new chapter was going to change my life forever, and I had my sights set on a happy ever after. Unfortunately, it didn't quite work out like that as I split up from my partner four months after finding out the news, she was pregnant. This was a mutual decision as we both agreed we would more than likely get on better apart than together however that decision took away my dreams of being a full-time Dad, and it took away the plans I had in my head for our future.

Once the baby was born, my ex-partner met someone else, so I had to deal with the fact that the baby also had two Daddy's in her life and it took me a little while to accept that, but nine years later I still enjoy having the relationship I do with my daughter, and I am able to see her whenever I can, and as it goes me, my ex-partner and her partner actually get on very well. So, although things didn't go as I had planned originally I know my daughter is happy with her two families (mainly because she gets two Christmas days and two Birthdays).

It is easy to have plans or visions of your future and for those plans to easily be taken away. I had a vision of being there when she took her first steps, when she said her first words and when she used the potty for the first time but instead, I just had to accept that wasn't going to be the case.

I may not have the perfect set up with her, and I wish I could see her more, but there are also a lot of positives our relationship brings as well. You may not have the perfect dog, and you may have initially had a vision of a nice family dog that you could take on nice long walks, cuddle up to on the sofa etc. Sadly visions and plans can change, and although you may not have the perfect life with your dog that you were expecting, there are things you can do and trust me when I say your dog may have certain issues, but I bet he has some great points too.

There is nothing more rewarding than adopting a rescue dog; however a lot of rescue dogs do come with certain issues. These issues could quite easily have developed due to neglect, abuse or both, and you need to be prepared for a potential challenging journey. With hard work, dedication and consistency, you have the potential to achieve a very loving and caring new addition to your family.

In the United Kingdom, it is estimated that 12 million households have pets with 25% of those households having a dog. Out of that 25%, 42% of owners report their dog as being aggressive towards other dogs.

This is a huge number which is why I tell all owners that have a reactive dog. **YOU ARE NOT ALONE.**

A lot of owners, not just the ones that have rescued a dog, struggle with this because it's certainly not what they signed up too when they first bring a dog home.

I was one of those owners. Let me tell you about my old dog, Lady, who was a beautiful German Shepherd. Lady grew up with other dogs, she used to love going to the beach and playing with other dogs… don't get me wrong she had a number of issues shall we say (I could write a whole book on Lady!) but one thing was for sure she loved interacting and socialising with other dogs.

As she started to get older, if I remember correctly, she was about 6/7 years old, and we were out on a walk at the beach. She was playing with one of her canine friends, Sasha, who she had played with on numerous occasions. It was very common for these two to play rough and chase one another. This one particular day, something out of the ordinary happened, after a few minutes of normal play Lady yelped and got into a scuffle with Sasha. At the time, I presumed Sasha must have nipped her during play and thought nothing more of it.

A few days later a similar incident between Lady and another dog occurred, and as the weeks passed, she was starting to do it to more and more dogs, and she got to a stage where she wanted to chase off other dogs that were approaching her. Naturally, I was thrown, and at the time, I thought could it be due to that one negative association with Sasha? After all, it can sometimes only take one negative association.

As a veterinary nurse and knowing the type of breed Lady was, I decided to take her to the vets to rule out anything medical. She had an x-ray, and it turned out she had arthritis. She was put on medication to help with the pain and inflammation, and after some training and positive reinforcement, I got her to a stage where she started to want to interact with her canine friends again.

It was a frustrating time though, especially with how out of the blue it all came. I found it incredibly difficult to walk Lady who was lunging, barking and often trying to attack other dogs.

As a dog owner, we have a huge responsibility, and that doesn't just involve making sure our dog is fit and well and providing them with what they need. We also have a responsibility for their actions as well.

I did not want to have to live a life of waking up at 4:30am to take Lady for a walk to avoid other dogs and their owners. I enjoyed my walks with Lady, and I enjoyed being out with her. I am a family man, and I enjoy being out during the day with the family, which included Lady. To have a reactive dog was not an option I was prepared to live with.

Unfortunately, that responsibility is too much for some owners, after all, it is difficult to deal with this behaviour problem. Throughout the country there are at a lot of dogs that end up in shelters due to their problematic behaviours towards other dogs. This is certainly something I found when I worked for Dogs Trust. Some owners find it incredibly difficult and they feel they have exhausted all options and the reality of owning a dog like this proves to be too much so rehoming or sending the dog to an animal shelter is sometimes the easiest option.

Sadly so many dogs in shelter get euthanised and although in a lot of cases this is a last resort it breaks my heart as sometimes, a little bit of hard work and regular training will help to correct this problematic behaviour. No doubt you want to do the very best you can for your new rescue dog, and if you are prepared to put in the work and accept the potential challenging times ahead, then you will, trust me.

I work with a number of reactive dogs on a daily basis, and I hope what I am about to share with you will help with your new rescue dog.

Before you can stop your dog from lunging, barking, snarling or just generally acting problematically around other dogs, there is one very important question you need to ask yourself and that question is WHY?

In order to correct a problematic behaviour, you firstly need to understand WHY your dog is reacting the way he is, only then can you truly do something about it.

As humans we are able to explain to one another the emotions we are feeling (sometimes maybe we do not handle it as well as we could i.e. we shout or we slam doors) unfortunately dogs do not have that luxury which is one of the reasons I think so many owners get stressed and frustrated when it comes to owning a reactive dog.

Before we look at the main reasons why your dog is reacting the way he is around other dogs I am going to start by telling you one of the reasons your dog is NOT reacting the way he is.

As a canine behaviourist, owners have the option to book a free 15 minute telephone consultation so that we can discuss the issues the owner is experiencing with their dog whether it be behavioural or training, but there is one thing I hear at least three times a day; "my dog is being dominant!"

The dominance theory

The word dominance is a word I very rarely use, and when I hear someone say it, I know I have my work cut out as sadly so many people believe their dogs are trying to dominate them, trying to take over the house, trying to be dominant around other dogs.

If you look at the definition of the word 'dominant' in the Collins Dictionary, this is what it says

"Someone or something that is **dominant** is more powerful , successful , influential , or noticeable than other people or things."

Answer me this, why on earth would your dog want to be more powerful or successful than you? Correct me if I am wrong but do you feed your dog? Do you walk your dog? Do you buy your dog new toys, treats? If your dog does any of the above, then please give me a call, I would love to hear about it!

Why would a dog want to dominate you when you provide everything for them? When you start to think of it like that it now seems a bit silly, doesn't it? (I can hear you saying "Yes Tim"). The issue with the dominance theory is so many owners believe that their dog is trying to achieve higher social 'status' therefore to correct this, the owner needs to establish 'dominance' over the dog and implement it as part of their training plan…. WRONG!

I can all but guarantee that implementing the dominance theory will end up, resulting in one thing…you getting bitten…dog gets put to sleep! I hate to be so black and white, but I see and hear this day in, day out.

I will always remember a rescue dog I did an assessment on, a lovely little spaniel called Bluey. From the history given by the owners, Bluey was displaying aggression around certain toys, chews and he hated going in the car (he only went in the car to go to the groomers) and they sought the help from a 'trainer' who advised that they must show Bluey who is boss! The so-called 'trainer' visited the owner's house for an appointment and apparently after speaking to the owner Bluey growled at the trainer and then hid behind the sofa.

The trainer then grabbed Bluey out of the sofa by the scruff of the neck (sounds like a lovely person right) and explained to the owner that this behaviour was not acceptable and that he needed to show Bluey who was in charge.

The trainer shouted, and Bluey at this point, wet himself purely out of fear. The trainer advised the owner to implement a training programme which followed the dominance style methods of training and guess what happed…. the owner got bitten time and time again, and the dog lost all trust and confidence in her, and she lost all trust and confidence in her dog.

She finally got in touch with me to which I was appalled by the training tips (if you can call them that) that she had been advised to implement and it took a very long time, and lots of hard work before Bluey started to trust his owner with the help from someone who actually knew what they were talking about and someone that used up to date proven methods of training (positive based methods of training).

Imagine if our lives were lived in a way where we tried to dominate our partners (I wouldn't stand a chance with my wife!), that is not what a relationship is built on. A relationship is built on trust and love.

I will always remember watching Coronation Street (That's right, I'm a soap man) back in 2012 with the domestic violence storyline between Tyrone Dobbs and Kirsty Soames. I personally found it very difficult to watch, but unfortunately, we do live in a world where this happens.

The vulnerability and fear displayed by Alan Halsall, who plays the character Tyrone, was incredible. The way this storyline was delivered helped a lot of people come forward and speak out. That is something we have the luxury of, a voice! Unfortunately, dogs don't have a voice and spend a lot of their life in fear as owners attempt to inflict the dominance theory.

No dog should have to live a life of fear!

So where did the dominance theory come from and why do so many people still use it?

Back in the 1970s, there was a study carried out on wolves in captivity. Now it is important to remember that these wolves were not related and they were all placed into one enclosure and observed for behaviours. The evidence gathered showed that these wolves fought over resources such as food, sleeping areas and mates and the studies suggested that there was a hierarchy system in place with the 'Alpha' (the leader) having first dibs at everything.

Therefore they were branded as a dominant species, and because dogs were believed to have descended from wolves, then they too were branded as a dominant species that were trying to take over our households and be the 'Alpha' of the pack….what a load of dog poo!

How many of you watch Big Brother? Back in the day, when I had very little to do (you know before marriage and before children when you seem to have more time to yourself), I used to enjoy watching Big Brother but what happened? What made it good TV? A bunch of strangers were placed in this one house and viewed by millions of people but let's be honest what kept us gripped the most? The arguments, the bitchy comments, the moaning! Strip that all back and what were the arguments, the bitchy comments and the moaning all over… Resources!!

The creators of Big Brother knew this, which is why limited supplies of things were placed in the house, to encourage arguments and why… because that makes good Television! If you look at this scenario of the Big Brother house then surely it makes sense as to why these unrelated wolves in captivity also displayed the behaviours that they did… not because they were dominant but because they were stressed, they were frustrated!

Very recently, with thanks to modern technologies we are now able to get up close to wolves in the wild (I love a bit of David Attenborough!) and there is now no evidence to suggest that wolves are a dominant species they live very similar to the way we do as a family and they work together as a family to ensure the survival of the pack.

I am sure you have heard 'trainers' mention in the past about how you need to establish the alpha role within your household if you want to have a better-behaved dog. Let us have a look at some of the methods of training that these 'trainers' advise people to implement and you let me know your thoughts!

· Pin your dog down to the floor if he is 'misbehaving' and hold him there until he is calm

- Eat before your dog
- Leave a room before your dog
- Be more assertive with your dog
- Take your dog's food away as they are eating, so he knows 'you are the boss'

You must agree this is ridiculous! The problem with the dominance theory (apart from it being a huge pile of dog poop) is it causes stress for your dog and in a lot of cases can cause fear. Please correct me if I am wrong, but this is not why we got a dog; we got a dog to be a part of the family and to be loved. I do appreciate at times when you are at the end of your tether you want results and you want results now, but I hate to break it to you that's not how it works with dog training. Dog training requires time, patience and consistency.

Now that we know and understand that our dog is not displaying dominant behaviours, let's have a look at a number of potential reasons why your rescue dog may react the way he does.

Inadequate socialisation

A lack of socialisation at an early age can lead to a dog that is fearful of people, dogs, experiences and new places. It is important to remember that early life experiences or should I say a lack of experiences can shape a dog's behaviour.

A negative experience

It is not uncommon for a dog who has been adequately socialised and has enjoyed in the past playing with other dogs to suddenly become reactive, especially if he has had a negative experience with another dog i.e. been bitten or attacked.

Medical

I'll always remember when my wife was in labour, she said things to me, did things to me that I know she didn't really mean (I'll not share them with you as the pain is still there) but that is what pain can do to a person. It is exactly the same with dogs, but they only have one form of defence – their mouth.

Humans

It is true, unfortunately we too have a massive part to play in the way our dog reacts around other dogs.

We are responsible for a lot of our dog's bad habits, and unfortunately in a lot of situations, we actually reinforce a dog's problem by the way we react. We tend to do things such as scream and shout at the dog to 'behave' which in turn adds further negative arousal to an already negative situation.

I think one of the main issues us humans have is we are absolutely hopeless at reading dog's body language which in turn means we miss warning signals and before we know it, it's too late. Getting to know your rescue dog and paying attention to his behaviour is the first step you need to take to move forward. You can find out more about reading a dog's body language in my book, Help! My dog is a devil with other dogs.

Sadly a lot of the above issues may have been caused by previous owners before you rescued your dog, and you can't change those things. As the crazy monkey from The Lion King once said, "It's in the past, it doesn't matter", and to a degree, those words are true because our job now as the new owners is to help our dog so that they can continue to have happy and stress-free live in their new forever home.

To do that we need to implement a training programme to build up a positive association around other dogs as well as help to recondition those unwanted behaviours sadly your new rescue has been displaying. This is what I had to do with Lady, and I implemented a desensitisation programme to recondition the unwanted behaviours she was displaying as well as build up a positive association around other dogs.

This involved teaching Lady to 'watch' me every time she saw a dog. This was built up gradually; initially, I taught her the command indoors and then moved that to outdoors. I then started to use it around other dogs at a distance where Lady was non-reactive, and over time I decreased that distance until we got to a stage where I was able to walk past another dog without any dramas.

The key to remember when implementing this is to ensure each time the dog looks at another dog you immediately give the 'watch' command, and then you issue a treat as soon as the dog looks at you.

By doing this, you will recondition the unwanted behaviours, and over time the dog will start to associate seeing another dog with getting a reward, therefore, building up a positive association around other dogs.

If your rescue is reactive to other dogs and you want to find out more regarding what you can do to help, then pick up a copy of my book, Help! My dog is a devil with other dogs, available from Amazon. This will work you through a full training programme, and soon enough you will be able to enjoy your walks with no dramas.

About the Author

Tim Jackson

Tim Jackson started his career working with animals as a veterinary auxiliary nurse. He trained and qualified as a veterinary nurse in 2007 at Myerscough College. He was promoted to Head Veterinary Nurse and spent a number of years helping animals and their owners. During his time in practice, Tim also qualified as a canine behaviourist, allowing him to offer one-on-one training sessions for all problem behaviours utilising only positive, reward-based training programmes.

In 2008, Tim launched Pets2impress, a company that took the region by storm. What began as a pet sitting service soon expanded to offer a variety of services.

In 2013, Tim took the decision to leave his position as Head Veterinary Nurse to expand Pets2impress and to work towards opening a doggy daycare. In 2015 Tim opened a state of the art daycare facility, offering a safe and stimulating environment for dogs whilst their owners' are out at work. His experience as a qualified veterinary nurse, dog trainer and canine behaviourist gave him a comprehensive understanding that all dogs have different physical and emotional needs, allowing daycare sessions to be tailor-made to suit each individual.

Tim is well known for his sense of humour and love and dedication to the welfare of all animals. Tim has owned several animals over the years including a rescue tarantula (which he was absolutely terrified of), an iguana, bearded dragons, cats, hamsters, rats, mice, fish and dogs.

Tim's mission in life is to help owners who struggle with their anxious or fearful dog to prevent dog's ending up in shelter.

When not working Tim can be seen swapping Doggy daycare for Daddy daycare. Tim loves nothing more than spending time with his three adorable children. He can also be found out walking his dog Buddy and every now and then enjoys a nice pint at the local pub.

To find out more about Tim and Pets2impress please visit the Pets2impress website www.pets2impress.com

Emma Lee

Adopting a dog with a long shelter history

When I first started volunteering as a dog walker at our shelter in rural France, it was not long after the previous administration had collapsed and our current director had taken over. We'd just bid to host the municipal pound on-site which would bring us state funding, but prior to that, we'd run largely on donations and in very old-fashioned ways - more of a hobby than a shelter, really.

In many countries where there aren't organised charities running large networks of clean and well-funded shelters, we suffered from a lack of fundraising and also a lack of marketing that meant many of our animals were here for years. I couldn't understand why so many great dogs were still in kennels. Sure, they were lively and untrained on the whole, but that's what you get when you're kennelled for most of the day.

I didn't really get to grips with the scale of the problem until later in the year. We have intake sheets attached to all the kennels, but other than a quick name check and having a look if they had any quirks on the handwritten notes, I never really thought about how long some of our dogs had been around. Worse still, the kennel corridors were really badly lit, the intake sheets were photocopies of photocopies, and intake dates were written in tiny, faint letters.

Starting to take photos and share them on our ancient internet forum (who remembers those?!) I started to get a sense of the scale of the problem. I got a spreadsheet going and started to look at what was going on. With over four hundred animals on-site, including 160 dogs, over half of those dogs had been here for over two years. 44 had been on-site for more than four years. Two had been here for 11 years. How was it that so many dogs were languishing in kennels? It was an absolute travesty.

What became clear, right from the get-go, was that we could make use of social media. We started up a Facebook group and webpage and started sharing. Coupled with information about the kind of homes dogs could live in, we ran a number of campaigns to find homes for dogs. As long as we carefully matched dogs with homes, and as long as we were explicit about the kind of homes these dogs would need, we had loads of success. Two years later and it was a completely different picture. Four years down the line and we're able to take on dogs with behaviour problems or at risk of euthanasia in other shelters as well as managing our own population, which stays almost at a constant.

What has really helped is having families who've gone into adoption with their eyes wide open. You can't afford to be a bleeding heart when you take on a dog that's been in kennels for seven years. What we also found was that while some people occasionally need the adulation for taking on a 'rescue', most of our adopters of dogs with long stays were quiet, reserved and deeply practical.

I say 'rescue' because I truly believe that labels are often unhelpful. People don't refer to their cats, rabbits or chickens as 'rescue' animals although they too can have behavioural problems that are a side-effect of long-term living in stressful environments. Even our dogs of 11 years' hard time were, on the whole, 'second hand' dogs rather than dogs with complex behaviour problems. Some didn't like other dogs. Some were completely untrained. We had no idea if many had even lived in a home. Some had history where cats were concerned. But what we didn't need were people adopting dogs out of pity. For that reason, we kept photos out of kennels, tried to give a real sense of the dog, and we were clear in vetting homes to suit.

There are four things that make a good adopter for long-term dogs: ability, environment, intention and exertion. Author Simon Sinek always asks you to start with WHY… and that's important too for our adopters. You've got to have the right intentions, and that can't simply be to 'save' a dog. Why do you really want to adopt this dog? That can be a tough question to answer. You also have to have the other three factors too.

We didn't need expert dog trainers, where ability was concerned: we needed people who were prepared for dogs who might know little of house-living. These needed to be people with some experience, sure, and often it really helped if they'd rehomed dogs before. Love and patience aren't enough if you've never house-trained an adult dog. We needed flexibility and problem-solving, an ability to think on your feet rather than someone who'd done fifteen years of dog school. 15 years of dog school was a welcome addition, but we needed people who could cope with the unexpected.

We also needed people with the right environment. I'm a firm believer that one of the hardest things we ask a dog to do is switch from an environment they've known to something unfamiliar. Lots of stairs, small gardens, low walls, lots of neighbours and apartment living won't probably suit many of our dogs, so we needed people who had homes that were suitable for our dogs.

You could be living off beans on toast and have a tumble-down cottage in desperate need of renovation, but if you had good fences and time, the kind of life to suit a dog, then that also made things much easier. That's not to say that dogs who have lived in apartments don't need homes, but it's so much easier to match like with like. We also needed people who understood that these dogs might take time to adjust to freedom.

Finally, we also needed people who were able to exert a little effort if needed. Adopting a long-stay rescue when you have literally no spare energy or capacity is a recipe for disaster. If you need a dog to be quiet and settled because you've got to go out to work, you can guarantee they won't be. If you need a dog whose routine fits yours and who is settled at night, you can guarantee they'll be pacing at 4am and singing you the song of their people. Ironically, we found that most people never needed that capacity as long as they had it. We needed to provide a bit of 24-hour support, but that too was never needed when it was there.

It's a really good idea to meet the dog first if they're a long-stay dog or at least to work with a rescue that has the capacity to take the dog back if necessary. Although this is rarely used in our shelter, the fact that we can offer it is important. That means more than just paying lip service to support.

See the dog where you can and have an honest conversation about the dog's needs. You can usually tell what they're like: Are they sociable? Are they reluctant to approach? Are they barking at dogs and people going past? Are they a bit nuts but able to pay a little attention to you? If they've been there that long, the staff will know their quirks, for sure.

Then check your own ability. Can you physically manage the dog if they turn out to be the world's best car chaser? Can you cope with them and your own dogs if you have others? Do you have the skill to handle them if they do come with behavioural problems? Do you have the cash and the back-up if there are physical issues? Do you have the emotional reservoirs to cope with them too? For many dogs with long stays, they may have age-related issues that you can't just overlook in doing a good deed. Some rescues offer support for dogs like this, and that can be immensely useful.

Think about the home you can offer and if you need to, plan in advance. Baby gates, x-pens, hook and eye locks and fencing can all be really useful to bear in mind. Many trainers talk about having two levels of security for dogs that are a problem. I think the same is true of long-stay dogs as you simply won't know what their needs will be. Crating them may not be an option at all, and you have to think how they will cope in your pristine home if they're not house-trained.

Be honest with yourself that you may need to be 24/7 there for the dog for at least a few weeks - or to have someone who is. Be honest about how you'll manage life and work and visitors. It's okay to want an easy adoption - there are plenty of adoptable or rehomeable dogs who'll just slot right in - but choose your time carefully.

Finally, check your intentions.

One of our first long-termers to go was Smoke. This 13 year old husky cross had been at the shelter for 11 years. Although he had a series of exclamation marks by his name, nobody even knew why.

Having him in foster for a short time showed us that he was fine with other dogs and that he was a bit bemused by the world. Glass doors didn't make much sense to him, and he wasn't quite sure how or where to lie down. He literally stood up until he almost fell over in exhaustion.

His adoptive family had been warned that he didn't like grooming, grabbing or restraint, and they took that to heart. They couldn't have been more flexible, gentler or more capable. He lived out his retirement in the foothills of the Alps, giving in to renal failure some months later. Being prepared for a dog that never really bonds to you, and putting your expectations aside can be hard. Just 'being' around them with no expectations is so important. If I learned anything, it was that the people who take the biggest risks are the ones who have thought it through and who are prepared for anything. That can include both emotional and financial costs too. But after 11 years of shelter life, Smoke saw the beaches, and he saw snow. He went for walks and hung around with children. He found his bed, and even after 11 years in kennels, he was clean in the house. Long stays in kennels don't always mean more problems than short stay dogs.

As for my own girl Lidy, she came to me after three years in kennels. She's my newest canine family member. I have another old girl too, Flika, who had seven homes before me. In many ways, the number of homes can be more significant than the time spent in kennels.

Before Flika, Tobby was my last shelter guy who'd had 14 months at our shelter. Ralf and Amigo who'd come before were relative lightweights with only weeks under their belt. Like Smoke, Tobby had needed a little bit of reassurance about where to sleep and that it was okay to lie down. We have financial support for adopting oldies, which really helped, but he needed a bit of emotional support too: typical shepherd found it hard to cope without a flock, and so for the remaining 19 months of his life, he was never home solo.

Oldies can be enormously easy as long as they know where to sleep and what time grub's up. Flika was not so easy, as her seven former homes might testify. Both Tobby and Flika needed me to adapt. In most ways, their behaviour was always the same: I adapted, not them.

Flika is a social butterfly, and I'm still not sure if her supposed separation anxiety is really just Fear of Missing Out. I joke, of course, but if you don't have the energy, the ability or the lifestyle to cope with a 14-year-old Malinois who can eat through doors if you leave her, then that virtuous feeling about what a great thing you've done will go straight out the window about the third time your friends go out, and you're babysitting a destructive grandma who can't live without you. Again, I knew this before I got her: great relationships with the shelter or rescue are really useful.

Lidy was the most complicated of all. Not for nothing is she with me. She was surrendered as an 11-month old and quickly picked up a reputation at the shelter after a first failed adoption. It's really tempting to shame people or dismiss their stories when they surrender dogs, and I've often scoffed at her intake notes that said ok dogs, ok cats, ok kids, unless 'ok' means "Quite Like Eating Them With Crudités". But nothing I hadn't known. After all, I was the one reason she made it through 3 years without biting any other creatures. Asking myself if I had the ability was easy: if I could work with her in the shelter, working with her in the home was okay. The environment was tougher. Concreted fences are one thing, but it's not easy living in the middle of a rural area with a dog with insanely high prey drive. Plus the girls don't get on. I planned that they would live apart, and so they do. Forearmed is forewarned. With baby gates, screens and lots of enrichment, we get by.

Being prepared to adapt is crucial. It's never the things that you think will pose problems. Lidy also clearly suffered from anxiety too, and taking my two out for a walk became a nightmare. I'd planned to leave her 45 minutes in her well-fortified Fort Knox, but trying things out is always necessary. Turns out she's fine if she's inside and not fine if left in her own well-secured (and massively expensively fortified!) garden. That can be about ability too. Having a lot of enrichment activities, knowing which remedies would help and having the skill to address her issues means that we can all just about cope.

Most people would worry about things like house-training and destruction. It's usually not those things at all that cause problems in my experience. Lidy has had a couple of accidents, more related to separation issues, but is generally super-clean. You worry too about carry-over behaviours, like Lidy had had three years where she couldn't have bedding. She'd eaten her way through plastic beds and wooden kennels. She'd snatched bedding from my hands and thrown it proudly on the floor in the shelter.

Here, six months in, her only incident has been a surprising rampage through the underwear drawer that was never repeated, though she does still like to collect socks. It's not that rescues or shelters lie: I did that assessment myself. But stress, boredom and no attachment figure pop out in familiar ways, and for Lidy that was chewing and destruction.

I'd also never seen her play. She'd always had dog companions - although she was remarkably choosy. If they weren't handsome young men of the pointy-eared variety, she wasn't interested. But she'd always had a tense relationship with them and never truly interacted. I was prepared for jealousy, but not for her to try and play with my handsome pointy-eared young man. Prepare yourself for a journey, too, because you have no idea what they're capable of.

Ultimately, if it works, it'll depend on your ability to adapt, to problem-solve and to innovate if you need to. Perhaps unsurprisingly, our adoptions after long stays have usually needed less hand-holding than the dogs we've known less. Stress behaviours in kennels disappear, some central behaviours may evolve or remain, and you'll be surprised by the reality of the dog you adopt, despite all you might know about them. You'll be prepared for destruction, urination, anxieties, escaping and all sorts of issues, no doubt. But your real problems may be things you'd never thought of.

A wise friend of mine remarked that in having worked with child adoptions from foreign orphanages, often the children in orphanages who presented the most problems were ones who'd had loving families and had been surrendered as older children. They acted out in the orphanage because they knew how much they'd lost and they were suffering. On the other hand, the quiet, docile children often found it harder to adapt in the home because they were often the ones who'd never formed secure attachments in the first place.

Those dogs who spend a long time in shelters and maybe have some of those behaviours that might put adopters off are often the ones, it seems to me, are very similar, and a lot of dogs who find it hardest in shelters and turn to stereotyped behaviours or destruction are the ones who miss that human bond so much. Generalised anxiety and excessive fearfulness can be in many ways the toughest challenges to cross, and such dogs often really benefit from a confident canine companion wherever possible.

Be prepared too for it all to fail. That's tough because there's always so much riding on it. In over fifty fosters, I've only had four that I couldn't have lived with (although all four are happily living with their families) - two who barked through the night, one who hassled my other dogs and a dog who had extreme separation anxiety when I wasn't able to adapt my work life to match. There is no shame in trying and failing with long-stay dogs. At least people know for next time. It's another reason that connection with the shelter or rescue is not something that ends when the ink is dry on the contract.

Prepare for the worst and expect the best, the old advice goes, and that can't take you far wrong. Be honest about your intentions and the energy you can put in, your ability and your home life, and you'll be able to adapt where and when needed. Adopting a dog who's spent the most part of their life in a shelter can seem daunting, but for the most part, it's only humans who take note of those months and years.

About the Author

Emma Lee

Emma is a behaviourist and trainer working in rural France. She is a member of the board of trustees at the Refuge de l'Angoumois, a large open-access shelter. Taking dogs from both urban and rural settings, the shelter faces a number of social problems including the use of hunting hounds, gundogs, working terriers, guard dogs, protection dogs and 'status dogs'. Like many shelters, the refuge de l'Angoumois is largely funded by private donations.

refugedelangoumois.fr
www.woofliketomeet.com

Stephen Wylie

Home

It is all so strange here. I have no idea what I am supposed to do, even more importantly, I have no idea what I shouldn't be doing. One thing I do know though is that I love it.

Everyone is so excitable and seem pleased that I am here; the children love it when we play. Dad likes to take me out on the concrete before we hit the green grass of what he calls "the park." Whilst Mam cuddles me up on the comfy seat once the children go upstairs. She strokes the top of my head, whilst she stares at the strange box in the corner of the room that has all the moving pictures on it.

The boy is the most fun, he wants to run and scream, then run and scream, then run and scream some more. Of course, I want to join in, who wouldn't? I run and bark, chase and bark, then run some more. I don't care if I knock plant pots over, I don't even see the girl as I zoom around the garden following the high pitched cries of joy. It wasn't my intention to knock her over.

I got wrong then, it made me feel bad. I was only trying to make the children happy. How was I to know that there were rules and places I was not allowed to go. The last time I was anywhere like a place like this, I was kicked every time I lifted my head off the makeshift bed of old newspapers and cigarette boxes that shared the space in the garage with me. My world amounted to nothing else but that dirty place.

I took those beatings because I knew nothing else. I took them because, despite the pain and the blood, I loved him. I had no one else.

I love my new family more though. They don't treat me like that and being with them is so much fun. I miss them when they go, it's awful. I hate being on my own, it makes me feel afraid and vulnerable. I have spent so much time on my own already.

It is easy to tell the days that I am going to be left alone. That strange screech of a noise happens earlier than other days, instantly I run to the bottom of the stairs, as I am not allowed up them, I have already learnt that lesson. I wait to see who will come down first, knowing that the hustle and bustle of everybody getting up together and wanting to be in the one room at the same time will happen at any second. That is when the arguments start, also when I retreat into my bed under the stairs and pretend that I am asleep. I don't want to get involved in that. I cannot help but shake at the sound of the shouting. It reminds me of where I used to live.

We all have breakfast together, although they sit at the big bench and my food is put in the far corner near the back door. I keep glancing over my shoulder to make sure that they are all still there, counting them one by one, but I enjoy my food so much. Where I used to live sometimes, I'd go days without getting anything to eat. It's all so new getting it at the same time every day, now it is something that I look forward to. "He needs Routine." Mam always says.

The boy likes his cereal, he adores to look for the gift at the bottom of the box. The girl has her headphones on most of the time, that sometimes leads to another argument. They are both dressed in the same colours, on the chest of their jumpers is the same symbol, the cloth around their necks has the same stripy pattern.

The hustle and bustle begin again, as Dad picks up his briefcase and his car keys. He gives them all a kiss on their cheeks, Mam first, then boy, then girl who tries her best to avoid the contact. Then the sound of the car engine.

Mam hurries around and gets the children to put their coats on, then she too picks up her car keys. I hear the creak as the front door closes, then the sound of the smaller engine disappearing off the drive.

They are gone.

The sound of the birds, busy with their own morning outside, buses passing by the bottom of the street, the roar of an aeroplane as it flies overhead, then the house descends into the blanket of loneliness. I walk to my bed from the passage where I watched them all leave one by one and let out a little sigh as I slump onto the red pillow with little grey bones on it. I hate being on my own.

The man in the red van comes to the door. I don't know what he wants, but he comes every day at about the same time. As soon as I hear the engine come down the street, I am up out of my bed and racing to the front door. Waiting for him to attack, starting to pace the passage, then as he gets to next door, I start to circle frantically, yelping with excitement at the thought of seeing him off.

He is here, I can hear him open the gate. His footsteps get louder as he gets nearer my front door. I begin to bark, the pitch getting higher the closer he gets, then I lunge as he pushes his weapons through the door. I shred them all, the brown ones and the white ones. The ones I miss coming through the letterbox, I destroy as they hit the floor. I don't realise that I have caught more in my mouth than the letters, so I don't stop. Little multicoloured bits of cloth from the rug that lies on the wooden floor, gets stuck in-between my teeth, but I just keep on ripping everything up that I can. I am beyond control; this is more than just a game for me, it is a war against this intruder.

Very quickly, the man with the red van knows this is a battle he cannot win and makes his way back down the path. It is only when I hear the sound of the gate click shut and his footsteps disappear down the street to intrude somebody else's garden, that I come out of my frenzy.

It has only been seconds, but the carnage is there for the humans to see when they return. Nobody will get into this house without them being here when I am in charge.

Bits of paper, rags of cloth and splatters of my spit decorate the hallway as I return to the sanctuary of my bed under the stairs. Exhausted but proud as punch of my achievements, I drift off to sleep. I cannot wait to see how pleased they are to see what I have done when they come home.

Mam gets home first, with the children. I hear the car on the drive and rush out of my bed to the door once more. Unlike before though, I am excited and happy to see them, my family has come home, I have successfully protected the house. I stand just out of reach of the door for when it opens, feet buried in shreds from my previous venture to the door, my tail wagging as ferociously as my ripping had been earlier.

The look on Mam's face as she walks in is not what I expect at all. She stands there for just a few seconds, then bursts into tears. The children rush in after her, curious at what has made their mother upset. The horror on their faces is quickly replaced by a look that screams "get me out of here." Then they run past her and me, the thud of their feet ringing in my ears as they make their escape up the stairs to the safety of their bedrooms, two doors bang closed making me jump.

Mam grabs me by the collar and drags me outside into the back garden. "You can stay there till Dad comes home and sees what you have done." I can only just make out the word 'done' over the slam of the back door.

When Dad gets home, I hear them shouting at each other. Then Mam storms upstairs like the children did, and another door slam's shut. He doesn't speak to me, the only time I see him is when he slides a bowl of my tea out from around the door into the garden. He says nothing, he just delivers my food. Eventually when it begins to get dark, he lets me back into the house. He says nothing once more, shows me to my bed and then mounts the stairs, switching the lights off as he goes.

The sun begins to rise, just as I hear the screech from above. I have forgotten about what had happened yesterday, I am just excited to see them all.

One by one, they descend. Mam and Dad first, neither speak to me. Then the boy, he gives me a hug and tells me he loves me until Mam sees him and gives him a stare that means "come and get your breakfast or else." The girl comes down last, she doesn't speak to me either, she is too busy on her phone as normal, but she pats me on the head to let me know that she knows I am there.

They go through the same routine as yesterday, only as they leave the boy decides that it is too warm for his jacket just before he goes through the door.

"Come on." Says Mam as she turns the ignition and the engine roars into life. "We'll be late."

"Coming." The boy says, and he throws his coat onto the floor, right onto what remains of the expensive rug I half-devoured yesterday.

I retreat to my bed, but my eyes quickly spring open when I hear the red van trundle down the street. He is back.

I go through the same routine as yesterday, only this time I don't realise that the quarry in my mouth is the boy's coat. I rag it up and down, tearing it more and more every time I see white stuffing float out like the clouds in the sky. The buzz is immense, like nothing I have felt before. The more I shake my head, the more white fills the room. I hear the tears but don't associate it with what I am doing. I am so enthralled I don't even hear the postman leave. Long after he is gone, I continue my trail of destruction.

The small pile of shoes at the bottom of the stairs are next. I throw them into the air one by one, chewing at the pieces of string that hang from the fronts of them. Then the carpet on the bottom stair next to where they are kept grabs my attention.

I pull at the corner next to the wall, and a whole strip of it comes up in my mouth. I keep pulling and more becomes mine, the first step then the second, then the third.

After pulling up the carpet from six stairs, the wooden spindles that hold up the bannister grab my attention. Sinking my teeth into the dark mahogany wood, a rush of excitement reverberates through my body as I see the marks I have left. The family will love my decorations when they come home. So, I continue to chew, working my way nearly halfway up the staircase, until eventually, I need a drink and a lie down.

Reflecting on my morning's work from my bed, the feeling of satisfaction begins to fade away, replaced by anxiety as I remember the reaction of Mam and the consequences of last night. I shouldn't have done what I have done this morning, I will be punished again for sure. I just love them so much and miss them when they are not around. I hate being on my own, I am frightened that they won't come back to me, and I will become forgotten again.

My life up to this point has not been very enjoyable, I have never belonged anywhere, for the first time now I have a family of my own, I shouldn't have repaid them by doing what I have just done.

I lie in my bed for the rest of the day, shaking at the realisation of my actions and fear at the thought of facing the consequences.

People pass the front window, but I don't move. I stay silent with my chin flat on the floor.

When the laughing and chattering school children pass, I don't see them off like I usually do, I keep in my den under the stairs and don't move.

Then I hear Mam's car pull onto the drive, the sound of three car doors opening and closing with a bang. Footsteps and then the key turns in the lock. I begin to shake even more; I am so frightened I urinate where I am lying.

I hear the creak of the rusty door hinge Dad keeps promising to fix. The children are arguing with each other as they always seem to do when they come back from school.

Then I hear the shattering of a wine bottle as shopping bags fall to the ground and nestle in the remains of the boy's coat and the rug.

The children stop their confrontation. The entire world falls into a deafening silence.

About the Author

Stephen Wylie

SHAK was formed in June 2006 by Stephen Wylie after the sudden death of his beloved German Shepherd cross, Shak, from Lymphoma.

Uttering those fateful words 'never again' he decided he wanted to help in the world of rescue and sold his own business to concentrate on providing an alternative to the destruction that was happening in pounds all over the country.

It was whilst working in one of those pounds that Stephen quickly saw there were a lot of dogs who were troubled by the life they had led before ending up discarded. As a result, they were losing their lives simply because they had nowhere else to go and give them a chance.

Rising from that horror, the charity grew to provide a lifeline to so many wonderful dogs. Only taking in abused, neglected and abandoned souls or put to sleep cases at the vets, today SHAK takes care of 60+ dogs at any one time.

By providing sanctuary in the beautiful Northumbrian countryside just outside of Alnwick, Stephen and his team help its inhabitants to learn to trust and, as Stephen calls it "allows them to simply be a dog again."

The charity receives no government funding or grants, all its funds are self-generated through its shop in Blyth and from the wonderful generosity of its supporters.

In 2013 that Stephen wrote his first novel, It's A Dog's Life. The agonising tale of a Rottweiler being abandoned and ending up in a pound. Seen through the eyes of the dog itself, the author was able to introduce some of the characters and heart-breaking situations that he himself had encountered whilst working in rescue.

Stephen has since published two other books called 'Only Human' and 'The Castle' that deal with a man struggling with mental health issues and depression.

To see the work Stephen and his team do, please visit www.shak.org.uk. Or if you would like to donate or help in any way, then please send an email to shak@shak.org.uk. To get your own copy of any of Stephen's books, visit www.stephenwylie.com.

Suzanne Gould

Management Games for your rescue dog

Some days life just gets in the way, all the work you've done with your Rescue Dog to stop him from reacting at another dog can fly out of the window, and there are times where practising your new skills just isn't appropriate.

Real-life happens, dogs suddenly appear, kids on scooters, bikes, loud bangs all happen when you least expect them too, so I teach these games to show different ways you can manage your rescue dog when they are faced with something that might trigger a reaction.

Tizer is a rescued German Shepherd Collie cross who joins me on my walking adventures nearly every day. He used to bark while on lead if he saw another dog. Slowly over time, his mum and myself used Look At That (LAT) to get him to stop this reactivity. Some days there isn't so much as a peep out of him, and other days he has clearly got up on the wrong side of the bed because he just barks at the first sign of another dog.

Using LAT with Tizer isn't always suitable as we could be in a situation where we don't have a chance to put distance between us and his trigger. This where these games come into play, if I can divert Tizer's attention back to me before his trigger aka the dog that is too close, then the chances are high that Tizer will keep watching me instead of looking at the dog.

These fun games I am sharing with you I use nearly every day with both of my Old English Sheepdogs Ally and Erick, along with all the dogs I walk too. They also will help your rescue dog have fun and engaging walks with you, even if you don't have a reactive rescue, you can still play these and have fun with your dog.

Repetitive Games

These games are amazing for distracting your dog, for example, when his trigger that he is either scared, frustrated or excited by, is coming towards you. The games distract him from the trigger to focus on what is predictable. Repetitive games are designed to make the appearance of treats predictable, and if your dog knows a treat is coming, he will tend to focus on that.

Game One - The Yo-Yo

Imagine you're on a narrow path and your dog's trigger is approaching then you can play this game while standing to the side while it passes. Or for example, a common problem is an off the lead dog approaching you and your dog who is on lead, then you can play the Yo-Yo while throwing treats far away for the other dog to get. I have played it while standing between two parked cars in order to avoid something on-coming on the street.

How To…

Practice this in your home or garden, then when you're happy, start playing it on walks.

1. Get your dog to sit directly in front of you. (it doesn't matter if you have to reposition yourself to stand in front of your dog who is sitting)
2. Stand with your legs slightly parted and get several treats in your hand.

3. Say your dog's name so he will look at you, once he does show him, you have a treat and drop one treat between your feet.
4. Your dog will bob their head down to get it and then should look back up to you aka a Yo-Yo movement.
5. As soon as he looks back up, drop another treat. Repeat for 8-10 times

This is a continuous game with no pauses or breaks, dog looks at you, drop a treat, dog eats treat and repeat. If you are concerned the treat will bounce away or your dog won't see the drop (my dogs never see the drop because of the hair!), then instead of dropping the treat place it on the ground between your feet.

Game Two - The Side to Side Yo-Yo

If your dog is really good at the Yo-Yo or it is not distracted enough by it then you can alter it slightly to this.

1. Steps 1 & 2 as above

1. Say your dog's name so they will look at you, once they are, show them you have a treat and drop one treat out to your right-hand side.
2. Your dog will follow the treat to get it and then should look back up to you.
3. Soon as they have looked back up drop a treat from your left hand at your left-hand side. Repeat for a 8-10 times.

Your dog is now moving side to side in front of you. Dog looks at you, right side drop, dog eats, dog looks at you, left side drop, dog eats the treat and repeat.

In a real-life situation, keep playing until your dog's trigger has passed by. Also make sure you play this game occasionally even when there is no trigger around, if you only keep it for when the trigger is around your dog, your dog will learn this game means their trigger is nearby.

Game Three - Look At Me To Win!

I love this game, it is in part an impulse control game but what it really does is teach your dog to give up looking at what he wants and look back at you. I used this game a lot with my dog Erick as he always had his nose to the floor following smells, it didn't matter if I was attached to him or not.

Tizer, used to run away in his former home, and this meant he'd spend days on the streets before being picked up and returned home. During his time on the streets, Tizer basically learned he could do what he wanted when he wanted, for Tizer this meant going up to every dog he saw, not a good habit to have when he's on lead. So I have used this game to help Tizer stop being so focused on going up to each dog he sees.

How To...

You need your really good treats. You can play this inside or outside.

1. With your dog sitting beside you on his lead, keep a hold of it and show your dog you have a treat in your hand.
2. Throw the treat out in front of you, it must be further than the length of your dog's lead. (Initially, it must be clearly visible to you dog so avoid throwing it in long grass etc.).

3. You must stand still. Your dog is likely to follow the treat in a bid to eat it. Keep a hold of the lead and make sure your dog doesn't pull you forward. He can go to the end of his lead.
4. Your dog will likely watch/stare at the treat, let him. You are waiting for the moment your dog stops looking at the treat and looks back to you.
5. As soon as he looks at you, say 'Good' and get him a treat from your pouch. It must be given in his treat spot.
6. Once he has eaten his reward, walk him up to the thrown treat and let him have it.
7. Repeat. Up to five times in a row.

This is a difficult game for your dog to play, so you must have patience, but your dog will get it. Play this often, when you are both comfortable playing in your home or garden, try and play it on quiet walks so your dog can learn in varying degrees of distraction. He is learning to check in with you in order to get what he wants.

Game Four - Positive Interruption

This is a skill I have always used with the groups of dogs I walk, I just didn't realise it had a name. A positive interruption is a way to get your dog's attention when they are too excited to hear their own name, I know that sounds a little backwards. Seriously sometimes your dog either having the time of his life playing or he could be reacting to his trigger, and saying his name gets no response.

Instead making a noise that is distinctive, that your dog rarely hears and he knows means good things, will get his attention really quick. As you're not shouting or reacting yourself, it's called a positive interruption, the equivalent of walking up to your dog and saying 'Excuse me could I have a moment?'

I use this mainly on my group walks when I can have up to six dogs off-lead playing, running and sniffing. All I have to do is make my Kiss-Kiss sound, and I immediately get the attention of all the dogs. I use it when I want to interrupt Tizer when he is barking his head off at another dog and paying no attention to the rest of the world.

How To...

Pick a noise to use. I make the kiss-kiss sound. You could pick a horse click with your tongue, saying yippee, whatever you pick, make sure it's distinctive and easy to replicate. Practice in your home, to begin with.

1. With your dog beside you make your noise and give him a treat.
2. Repeat up to 8 or 10 times.
3. Pause and wait for your dog to look away from you then make the noise. He should turn back to you straight away when he does give him a treat.
4. Then start to make the noise at random times in the home, ideally when your dog is doing something else i.e. play, sniffing, lounging around etc. reward when he looks at you.
5. Start looking for opportunities to use it outside in the garden, on your walks, whenever there are slight distractions around.
6. Keep practising this although try not to wear it out.

This sound is the cue for your dog to stop doing what he is doing and look at you. Once you have his attention, offer him a treat and then ask him to do something you'd rather they'd be doing. So, if your dog barks at the window, on walks or is too focused on a trigger, you can use this noise to interrupt him.

JUST REMEMBER - THIS WON'T TEACH YOUR DOG NOT TO DO SOMETHING IT ONLY INTERRUPTS HIM SO YOU CAN MANAGE THE SITUATION.

A Scared Dog

It is completely understandable for a lot of dogs who've either had a sheltered upbringing, lived in a foreign country or lived in wildly different circumstances could find elements in our lives scary. It could be noises, objects, people, animals etc. the trick here is to support your dog through it.

My dog Ally, after having a sheltered puppyhood, can be quite a scared dog. If she doesn't understand what she is seeing, she will automatically lower her body, and I'll hear a low growl, she is trying to work out if she should kill it or run away.

I remember being stood in my bathroom tidying when all of sudden I could hear Ally start growling in the next room. I went to see what was going on to find her with her lowered body growling at my backpack. I use a backpack for work every day, at the end of every day its dumped-on top of Ally's crate, emptied and repacked. Normally it laid down on its back; however, this time, it was sat upright, and that freaked her out.

I told Ally it was OK. I went to pick up the bag and popped it on the floor for her to inspect in her own time. She slowly moved closer and for every step nearer she heard “Good” from me; eventually, she relaxed, was sniffing the bag and wagging her tail. Any time she comes across something scary, and it is safe, I will let encourage her calmly to get closer and praise her for her braveness.

If you find you have a scared dog, support him, reward him for being brave even if it is the smallest step forward, watch for his body relaxing. Just be with him.

NEVER EVER force your dog to interact with something he is scared/frightened of. Don't turn his fear into an amusing game for yourself - oh yes, that does happen - because you will only be creating more serious behaviour problems later on in your dog's life.

Game Five - SH*T ITS GONNA GET ME!

This is a way you can help your dog find strength and confidence around unfamiliar objects, helping him overcome his fears little by little. I play this in my Rescue Dog Classes, and it's lovely to see dogs become braver.

How To...

1. Grab a selection of objects/items and arrange them on the floor in a safe place like your living room.
2. Let your dog in the room.
3. For any item he sniffs, looks at or walks towards praise him.
4. Be encouraging - if there is something he really doesn't like, you can calmly interact with it, so your dog can see you.

Items I gather up are Cardboard boxes, Plastic Bags either flat or filled up with safe dog items, traffic cones, hula hoops, dog agility tunnel, plastic bottles, kids' toys that make noise and so on. Use your imagination with objects and sounds, just don't do too much at once and above all remain calm yourself.

At The End Of The Day….

- Use whatever game or skill you have at your disposal with your dog to help avoid him reacting.
- Avoid shouting at your dog if he is reacting or being over-excited.
- Managing your situation with your dog is just as effective as using LAT.
- If your dog is scared, then support him, don't rush him.

About the Author

Suzanne Gould

Suzanne specialises in training for rescued/adopted dogs which is inspired by her personal history of adopting Old English Sheepdogs. After working with an increasing number of adopted dogs, whose owners were struggling as their dogs are considered reactive, don't listen or are scared by people, Suzanne earned the name of The Rescue Dog Ranger™.

Suzanne shows owners how they can transform their lives with their dogs. The training she provides isn't your typical obedience style; instead, she focuses on confidence building, strengthening communication and how to handle stressful situations.

To grab her book 'The Rescue Dog Rangers Roadmap', or get further information about Suzanne's services head over to www.edinburghholisticdogs.co.uk

Adam Delderfield

My Best Friend Martin

When I won dog trainer of the year in 2019, everything really came together on the last two days. This wasn't a fluke; it was because the first three days I didn't really do much of what you would consider 'training'.

I spent the first three days just making friends with the dog I was working with. This is why I recommend you don't do much 'training' with your new rescue dog in the early days either.

Now that might sound a bit wishy-washy, but I promise there is a reason for it. Let me tell you a story about my best friend to help explain.

My best friend Martin, by his own admission, could be a bit of a liability at times, especially when we were younger. I still remember when we first met, he was the new kid being shown round the school, and as our eyes locked across the canteen, I knew I would hate him. Well, it turns out I was right.

We had a few mutual friends, but this guy really knew how to push my buttons, he was the king of wind-ups, regularly doing or saying annoying things just to get a reaction. He was never a bully, just a teenage boy that didn't like living by the rules, and he always wanted to push the boundaries.

Is Martin reminding you of any dogs you know, yet?

The first year knowing Martin was hard work, but with the lowest of lows comes the highest of highs. We had both been allocated food technology for GCSE, and as there were only three boys in the class, me and Martin had been sat together. You can imagine my disgust when I walked into class, saw there was only one seat free and next to it was Martin, with the biggest grin on his face. The sudden realisation of having to sit next to him for two years sunk in.

At this point in our 'friendship' I wouldn't have done anything for him, he constantly wanted to borrow a pen or borrow ingredients he had forgotten. I was still convinced he was doing it on purpose to annoy me.

Later that day during lunch break, we were hanging around with some other mates, and a group of kids walked past and pushed into me. Before I had even managed to get my balance, Martin had jumped in and stood up for me.

I couldn't believe that out of all the people I was with, it was Martin who stood up for me without even skipping a beat.

Up until that point I always thought him winding me up was because of some sort of dislike he had for me, but in that moment I realised it was just because he wanted to have a laugh and was trying to get me to loosen up a bit and join in.

From there we became best friends and although he was still a pain in the arse, understanding him and knowing him a bit better, meant it all made much more sense.

Following school, our friendship had highs and lows. He was always the one most likely to get into trouble, get lost on a night out. It's like trouble follows him around. But he wouldn't be Martin if some sort of bad luck didn't follow him around.

Many years ago, we had got into an argument and not spoken for ages. I have no idea what it was about now, but I think it was a number of things he had done. I hadn't heard from him in a while, and I knew he was having a rough time with his partner.

Well, it was late at night, and my phone rang, whenever you see a late-night call from Martin you know it's not going to be good news. He had split up from his partner and was living back at home, but he had a massive argument with his family and was pretty much out on the streets. So, I told him he could come and live with me and my partner while we worked out what to do.

He ended up staying with me (Rent free, not that I'm bitter about it) for 6 months. But eventually, he got a place of his own and a new job. Now after that, he always used to ask me *Why Adam? Why did you take me in? Why are you still friends with me?* The answer… history.

We had a history together.

If a stranger in the street asked me to borrow my phone, I'm obviously slightly apprehensive, but I have no problem with my best friend borrowing my phone.

That's because we have a history, and a certain amount of 'trust' has built up between us.

I see this mistake being made so often when people get a new dog. Whether a rescue or even a puppy, there needs to be a long history.

A history of trust, choice, play and friendship. It's very tempting to try and train the dogs straight away, so you can immediately turn them into the dog you want them to be.

But one of my key mottos is *'in order to get the dog you want; you have to train the dog you have'*.

That's such an important statement because you need to work out what makes your dog tick and accept that the training might not look the way you thought it would. Although you might love your new dog, and care about it, just a few days or weeks of affection doesn't mean you are going to be the best of friends.

Remember how mine and Martins friendship started? Initially, his attempts to make me laugh and be my friend were seen as annoying, and it took years for us to become best friends. But we can do a lot better than it taking years to become best friends with your dog, so I have some top tips to fast-track your friendship.

Treat all dogs as individuals

Currently I have two dogs, and this first tip couldn't be summed up better than with my two. They are complete opposites; Chester is three and has enough energy to be a fully-fledged working dog. Chester loves fast-paced games, high energy exercise and is the most confident dog I've ever had. The moment I open one eye in the morning, I can hear his tail wagging, ready to start the day and go for a walk.

Buddy, however, loves to sleep and even at the weekend and I get up late, I still have to wake him up and try and convince him to come out. If I try and run with him, he actively slows down. If I go for a run with Chester, I'm dying at the end, and his mouth isn't even open, he looks at me as if to say, *'Right now the warmup is done when do we start running?'*

You have to start with an open mind and treat each dog as a blank slate.

Work out what they like

At trainer of the year, one of the dogs I worked with would hardly work for any of the treats we had, but on day three I finally worked out that he loved treats *and* loved training as long as the treat was soft and small enough for him to not have to chew.

He ate dry kibble as fast as lighting in a bowl but wouldn't touch it from your hand or any other form of treat that required chewing. You have to test every type of treat and every type of toy you can think of.

I specialise in recall and off-lead dogs, and this is something my students constantly hear. Don't let the pet shops decide what is a good treat or a good toy, *let your dog decide.*

Anyone who has ever had a puppy will tell you that pups would much rather eat your slippers or your dressing gown rope than the knotted rope toy that you brought specially for them. I get my students to think outside the box when it comes to treats and toys. Try something you've made yourself or found on a walk. If your dog likes it, and it's safe to use it, then use it.

Teach them to play and have fun

Play is such an important part of being a well-rounded and confident dog. My dog Buddy was run over by a cyclist when he was about a year old, and it massively knocked his confidence, he was far more aware of joggers, men and HATED cyclists.

I had to reteach him to play outside. From a dog that would happily play fetch or tug to a dog that was constantly looking over his shoulder and acted like I was trying to trick him when I got a toy out. So, I sat down, thought about what he liked and came up with a plan.

Now he loved soft ground like bark or gravel that he could skid around on, so I started taking him to the local park every day and playing tag.

Yep, I was a weirdo chasing my dog round the local kids' park.

I should probably point out that I went there in the mornings when it's empty.

Then I used the game of chase as a training technique, I would chase him and wind him up, then ask him for a sit, and reward him with another game of chase. Over time the play and games that we did on the walk changed the way he felt about walking, and he started to look forward to going out again. The scary bikes were less of an issue, and the other distractions didn't seem to distract him anymore.

The drive to work is more important than the work

When I first started work, my dad always used to say before I left, better to be late than not make it at all. This is because I had a motorbike and the last thing you want to do is rush, have an accident and never make it to work.

I take the same approach with rescue dogs when training, and it's such an overlooked part of dog training. Often, we are so transfixed on the dog that we want or think we should have that we are constantly thinking about how we can get them to be the dog we know they can be.

If you rush sometimes you can make mistakes and lose the trust and confidence, it is more important that you have a dog that wants to train, play or work with you. The desire to want to train is more important than the perfect recall or the best sit-stay.

All of that will come, but you must remember to train the dog in front of you to get the dog you want.

About the Author

Adam Delderfield

Adam Delderfield is an award-winning dog trainer from Milton Keynes. When the internationally respected *School of Canine Science* launched its Trainer of the Year award in 2018, it put his unique approach to the test. Convinced that his dog training methods could get the right results quickly and positively, he set out to prove it.

Working with three amazing rescue dogs from Battersea, including a 12-week old puppy, he fought off stiff competition from some of the UK's most experienced trainers to win the award. It was practical, indisputable proof that his approach really works.

Before becoming a dog trainer, Adam worked as an IT Major Incident Manager. His role was to support the IT Systems 24 hours a day 365 days a year, for one of the largest Retail Banks in the UK. Often the question comes up about how Adam went from high powered and very high-stress role in Major Incidents to dog trainer. The transition wasn't as drastic as you might think. Every day in Major Incidents, the job requires you to think on your feet and resolve problems as quickly as possible, which is what he does every day when training dogs. When presented with a dog training problem, he uses his expertise and experience to come up with the quickest possible solution.

Another big part of Adams approach is that he doesn't just fix the issues, he looks at the root cause, identifies what caused the issue to occur in the first place and then makes sure that he is putting information out there to help other owners prevent problems from occurring in the first place.

To find out more about Adam and Delders Dogs go to his website www.DeldersDogs.com.

Check his blog out and watch out for his new ebook *'The 3 Big Recall Mistakes – A Recipe For Disaster'*. Don't let your rescue dog off-lead until you read this guide!

Sarah Bartlett

Monkey see monkey do!

The trials of bringing a rescue dog into a multi-dog household.

I was all of 19 when I took on my first rescue dog. I already had two dogs at home – Bella a Rottweiler mix, and Ziggy a little dachshund.

I had been volunteering at Manchester dogs home taking dogs out for walks. There was one particular dog who kept getting overlooked, not by just by people looking to adopt but by the other volunteers too. This dog kept getting kennel cough and being moved from kennel block to kennel block. I couldn't help but fall in love with this elderly and slightly senile chocolate and tan Doberman who really could have given a Sea Lion a run for his money with his bark!

I brought him home for the day to give him a break, a day turned into a fortnight fostering and well, I failed at fostering.

He got to rest his old bones at Casa de Bartlett (technically Casa de Roper back then) for the rest of his days.

Rolo - the senile, 'bark like a seal' Doberman taught me so much, and despite his many quirks, I still miss him all these years later.

When he was at the dog's home, he was kennelled with other dogs, and he appeared to get on fine with them. He took to Bella and Ziggy straight away at home, and I didn't think much more of it. Well, that was until I took him out with the other two on a walk and he started to bark and lunge at other dogs. If he was off-lead, he was hard work anyway as he was going deaf, so recall was far from reliable, to make matters worse he would chase other dogs off and be an overall pest on the park – not exactly what I was used to or expecting!

I couldn't understand it, if he was fine with my other dogs and fine with dogs in the kennels why would he not like at least most dogs on walks?

This was before I was working with dogs professionally, and although I have to say I was pretty obsessed with dogs even back then, in reality, I didn't know much. Bella and Ziggy had only joined me the year before, so I had only been a dog owner for a year in real terms. The dogs I grew up with didn't really count, great memories of course and all rescues but let's face it parents bear the brunt of most things when we are talking family dogs, and we aren't as switched on or responsible.

Little 5ft nothing me at just 19 years of age walking two big dogs and a little one was a challenge in itself too. Adding the pulling, lunging and barking at other dogs didn't make walks fun at all. I resorted to a halti type head halter and a muzzle with Rolo to ensure I could still exercise him and safely for all involved.

I'm not going to share with you the ins and outs of the reactivity side that's not a story for now. I wanted to share with you what knock-on effects Rolo's dislike for other dogs had.

Bella started to copy what Rolo did.

Bella took a dislike to other dogs on walks, and it made me feel very deflated, ashamed and embarrassed to take them out. I had no control, and there were times I started to wonder if I had done the right thing adopting Rolo.

That's not to say I didn't love him; oh I loved the bones off him and would regularly defend him when friends would quite often make negative remarks toward him or try to suggest that I had taken on more than I could chew.

The comments didn't just come from friends either, but from other people out on walks, the 'you want to train those dogs' and ' who's taking who for a walk?' comments and my response of 'well he's a rescue' didn't do much, besides, Bella wasn't a rescue so my argument was null and void.

Rolo was only with me for around six months before he passed away. I am pleased I managed to give him a great final few months as I honestly believe he would have spent his remaining time in kennels if I hadn't brought him home.

Even after Rolo went over the rainbow bridge Bella's ASBO type behaviour still continued, and that caused its own issues, especially with how my life changed rapidly after and also the addition of another puppy but again a story and lesson for another time.

Dogs speak dog… 'Well duh' I hear you saying!

They are ever so in tune with what the others are doing and will more often than not copy all the worst stuff – very rarely the good.

Anything that involves excitement, adrenaline etc. such as barking, chasing, jumping and such like the other dogs are hard-wired always to join in - it's fun!

Fun for them maybe, but not for us and it makes life so much harder.

Taking on a rescue dog I think it's pretty safe to assume they will likely have some issues, and things that we try to help them with when we bring them home.

Often the dogs you have at home may have some minor issues that niggle you, but they are just that – niggles.

No dog is perfect, I would never expect perfection. I am far from perfect, but I truly believe that there are dogs that are perfect for us.

I titled this chapter Monkey see, monkey do, and I say that with a smile – it's not derogatory.

Dogs copy, they join in with their own species, and that often works against us if we aren't careful.

The following issues with existing dogs are the most common that if not dealt with before a new dog is introduced, will become a problem when the new dog joins in.

I cannot stress this point enough as it's the most common category I am faced with professionally with multi-dog households.

Any of the following may only be mildly annoying with one dog but guaranteed to become a real nuisance when adding more dogs to the mix.

- Barking at the doorbell
- Pulling on lead
- Not coming back when called off the lead
- Barking in the garden

- Barking at people passing the house
- Any inappropriate barking other than listed above.

It's worth mentioning that all dogs need to express normal behaviour, and this includes barking, usual barking would be barking to alert you of someone at the door or to alert you to an intruder or visitor, barking in excitement (within reason) and vocalizing during play. The more dogs you have, the more barking and noise you can expect, this is fact, but we do need to be mindful of visitors, neighbours and the dogs' excitement levels.

- Barking, lunging, aggression or frustration toward or other dogs when on lead or off. The same goes for the opposite issue – your dog being fearful and trying to run away from other dogs when on lead or off, same applies to people or livestock
- Chasing lunging or fear of traffic, people, cyclists, joggers, children
- Jumping up on people, either out on walks or visitors to the house

Solutions and management pre new arrival . *Though my guess is you already have a new rescue if you are reading this.

If your dog has any of the issues I have described, I would urge you to get help from a qualified professional trainer or behaviourist to at the very least improve it before newbie comes home. Honestly, the money, time and effort you put in now will be well worth the investment and save you a dog's lifetime of stress and frustration. And if the issue you are facing is a real bugbear, whatever you have been doing to 'fix' the problem apparently hasn't worked so far, or it would not be an issue now… harsh I know but true.

Birds of a feather flock together

Proper dog training means setting a dog up for success, and not setting them up to fail.

You will be setting yourself up to fail if you don't tackle whatever issues you are currently faced with.

You are the company you keep.

A chain is only as strong as its weakest link...

Yep, some old cheesy quotes, but this is your furry family we are talking about. Guaranteed if just one dog likes to bark more than the others, the new one will join in, because that's what dogs do! They will not look at the calmest dog and follow that one and copy its behaviour. Having calmer or nice role model adult dogs will give you the best chance to train puppy to do the same.

Management

Better to be alone than in the wrong company

Management is about manipulating the environment/situation and protecting the puppy from being exposed to unwanted behaviours performed by the other dogs. Or protecting the dog that is being managed from performing unwanted stuff.

Management is not training, but it is an extremely useful tool. In some cases, a management solution to a dog not coming back off-lead would be to keep the dog on lead, or if a dog is reactive or barking at other dogs, the management solution would be to avoid other dogs.

While none of these solutions are 'curing' the dog of the issue, it is preventing the dog from practising the wrong behaviour. This provides a window of opportunity to work on replacing the unwanted behaviour with a new and desirable behaviour as and when you can control the environment and set the dog up for success. Without management, as part of any behaviour modification plan, you will fail.

Just like us if we want to break a bad habit, it isn't productive to go back to the old habit between practising the new habit.

For example, let's look at smoking, when a person quits smoking, they try to replace the time that they would smoke with something else, this may be having a mint, or distracting themselves in some other way while the cravings are at the forefront of their mind. If they sometimes had a cigarette and sometimes didn't, you wouldn't consider them to be an 'ex-smoker' would you?

A dog who has practised a behaviour just a handful of times is a lot easier to train to do an alternative behaviour, than a dog who has had years and years of practising the wrong thing on what could be a daily basis. Patience is key, remember that training takes time and management solutions will help you in your journey to success.

Here are my top tips to ensure success when introducing a new rescue dog to your existing dogs.

1. Before you bring your new rescue home take a towel or blanket to visit them, rub it all over them (if they are happy with this, if not leave it with them for a day or two so they can lay on it) before bringing it home to your dogs. Leave it on the floor for your dogs to investigate and sniff (please do not put this on a bed for them), and do the same for

the new rescue dogs, they can investigate each other's scents and learn about each other without the pressure of being face to face this way. Although yes you will be carrying the scent both ways on your clothes, by doing this you are also making the scent familiar at home and setting all dogs up to almost know each other without meeting.

2. Don't rush the initial meeting with your established dogs at home! Take the dogs for a walk first, before bringing the new dog into the house. Ideally, have another person to handle your existing dogs, and you walk the new one. Don't bring them nose to nose, walk them parallel with a gap between the dogs, ignore any barking or frustration from any of the dogs initially – remember we are not letting them sniff our meet each other that this point and they will soon settle. Walk them parallel so they can get a feel for each other out of the corner of their eye while they walk and sniff at their surroundings.

3. Set up your home to keep the dogs separate initially when you are not present or able to watch them. This might mean baby gates, crate, puppy pens or just in separate rooms. Plan for your new rescue to sleep apart from the other dogs.

4. Allow yourself, the new dog and your existing dogs time to adjust, you wouldn't expect to have a new housemate and be bosom buddies straight away, you can't expect your dogs to do this either, it's a little unfair.

5. Allocate time to dedicate to the new dog individually, separate walks, training and play, you need to bond with them individually, this makes training and managing multiple dogs so much easier. While you are doing this be mindful to ensure your existing dogs still get quality time with you without the new dog and you keep their routine as much as you can.

Remember, things will be difficult at times, give yourself a pat on the back for doing something so amazing and remember that things will take time to settle down.

How could I have managed the issues with Rolo and Bella?

I could have walked the separately, so Bella never got to see Rolo barking and lunging at other dogs. Another option would have been to go on walks with all of them together but only where I was sure we wouldn't see other dogs – of course, you can do a mixture of both too.

Remember, this is all about almost creating the situation so that Bella would have perceived Rolo as being perfect as she never witnessed him doing the wrong thing. I'm not saying walk separated forever but walking separately so I could have worked on Rolo's behaviour without the other dogs there would have improved everything when they were eventually walked together again and made life so much easier. Bella would have not got into bad habits this way either.

The more dogs you have, the harder this gets, and the more management you will need.

Don't forget your new rescue could pick up bad habits from your existing dog too – it works both ways.

Get to know your rescue individually on walks first before taking them out with the others, for a couple of weeks. Bond with them without the presence of the other dogs so you can set yourself and your furry family up for success – don't end up in the same boat as I did.

About the author

Sarah Bartlett

I'm Sarah Bartlett. I'm known as the Multi-dog Maven, and my speciality is helping dog owners enjoy a stress-free life with their dogs. I practice what I preach and currently have five dogs of my own but hoping to get a sixth very soon.

I have had fifteen dogs in as many years, and I have made every mistake you can think of in that time. Hard lessons learnt but all of which have shaped me to be the person and trainer I am today.

I started the award-winning company Hound Helpers Ltd in 2007 and spend my days helping dog owners both locally in Worcestershire and nationally.

In my spare time, I'm often competing with my Dachshunds in Obedience and KC Rally. I also love to ride and drive my fell pony Billy, competing in carriage driving trials when we can.

If you have concerns in your multi-dog household, please do reach out!

Drop me an email to sarah@houndhelpers.co.uk for a chat

Or Visit my website https://www.houndhelpers.co.uk/rescue-dogs to claim your free access to the TDR seminar I did all about introducing a rescue to your existing dogs.

Books by Sarah

Another Pup? - The comprehensive guide to adding to or becoming a multi-dog household

Puppy Prepared? - The roadmap to getting your dream dog

Karen Boyce

Bertie's Story – The Rescue White Highland White

"Exposure and experience is all, what counts."

Lovely Goyal, I Love the Way You Love me

One Friday morning in 2002 the phone rang at my home, a Wiltshire smallholding I shared with my partner at the time, and I found myself talking to a good friend Jacki Ferris-Woods, who ran the rescue organisation Westie Rehoming. I occasionally helped the charity out with behavioural advice, and I thought this was going to be another of those types of calls.

Little did I know this particular call would actually change my life.

My friend started to tell me about a six-month old Westie called Bert. A lack of foster homes at that time meant she was struggling to place him anywhere, and would it be possible for me to have him for now.

"Just a week", she told me.

Of course, my answer was *"Yes"*.

And of course, the upshot was that Bertie stayed with me for the next 14 years!

I did resist him though, and only finally had him microchipped in my name (in the days before compulsory microchipping) when he was about 7.

I jokingly told people that knew him that he was only now 'officially' part of the family.

However, like a lot of rescues, Bert came with some emotional baggage.

Bert the Westie had spent the first six months of his life in a flat. He was eventually rejected when he bit a toddler who got into his bed with him. Hey how weird is that? A terrier that used his teeth to tell someone to get out of his space. Believe it, this is not so unusual.

Bert was never particularly happy or trust-worthy with visitors indoors ever again; and indeed a few years later when moving to Wales, he spent the rest of his life happily living outdoors.

Bert was then as happy as Larry and became a bit of a local celebrity. Amongst other things, he was known for bringing the walkers to a halt as their dogs insisted upon paying him due homage, before he graciously gave them leave to move on!

Bert was also a shadow chaser. Now this behaviour is likely to happen when a dog is confined in one space and bored. He could have learnt this locked in a flat, but I have a gut feeling he was a puppy farm dog. It is so typical for a pup raised in a sterile environment to turn to amusing himself with the only environmental stimulus he has, shadows and reflections. Puppy farm pups can also be tail chasers and even in the extreme dip into self-harm.

There were some other tell-tale clues Bertie was a puppy farmed dog. He also had a soft coat, which a terrier shouldn't have, but a pet owner might prefer, and he was also bigger than average. Being a bit bigger has a great advantage for a puppy farm breeder as you can pass off a six-week old pup as an eight-week pup and get rid of it sooner. Money in the bank sooner and less money spent on food.

So is a Rescue Pup Likely to be Different Compared to a Normal Breeders Puppy

Well, the truth is YES, it most likely is. But this is a huge generalisation as I think of a normal breeder as someone with a nice mummy dog mated with a nice daddy dog and then raising a lovely litter. Of course, there is a huge range of average breeders in-between.

….. and average often isn't good enough!

Believe me also when I say that the price of the pup is no indication of a better breeder.

I have seen hundreds of puppies in my classes over the last two decades, and I am often shocked as to how a breeder thinks a litter should be raised.

So, why do we need to take more care with our rescue pup?

Well, unlike a 'reputable breeder' who will take time to match up a suitable bitch and dog for breeding, a puppy which comes from a less reputable breeder almost certainly wasn't bred for its temperament! Whether an accidental litter from people who don't care, a breeder breeding for cuteness to sell or a puppy farm breeder, breeding from stock which are confident and steady wouldn't ever have been a priority.

Timidity is a genetic trait not different to coat colour or size.

Perhaps the mother was treated badly, neglected, or abused during pregnancy. The research is clear that any stress will be passed onto the pups.

How bad breeding creates difficult dogs

Early or inappropriate weaning could likely have a pup with a lack of understanding re impulse control and/or coping with frustration. A good breeder has the mummy dog shutting down the milk bar sporadically around seven weeks and teaching the pups that they weren't born with a silver spoon in their mouths.

From my own experience breeding my own German Shepherd pups occasionally, it is a particularly enlightening time to see pups confused and frustrated. My own bitches often take to the high ground of the couch and smile sweetly down on whinging sons and daughters. The moment a pup gives up and wanders off is a pivotal point in its life; you see sometimes you just do not get, no matter how much you want something. Learning how to emotionally handle lack or removal of a reward is essential to all young animals.

Bad nutrition is also a key factor in the creation of poor physical and mental health in a puppy. Manufacturers continue to beguile owners with pretty pictures, videos, and words, whilst at the same time producing products with cheap fillers and poor-quality meat; all to ensure happy shareholders. Yes, happy shareholders! Whilst delivering "value" as another key area! But this can simply be just another word for simply meaning poor quality.

Lack of stimulation . Puppies who come through rescue are often raised in a sterile environment, and yes, I am afraid to say that even those raised in a rescue centre can suffer from lack of enrichment. This lack of stimulation limits brain development.

Lack of socialisation . Then there is the lack of human interaction. When I have a litter of pups, I invite all my instructors in to handle the pups from a very early age. Well behaved friends can also join in. I am looking to give my pups early positive experiences of people as early as from the age of 3 weeks, as up to 12 weeks puppies are primed for bonding to other animals and individuals. They are also primed to learn that people, objects, and environments are safe, and to start understanding the body cues and signals they see from humans and other animals. This is their **SENSITIVE PERIOD,** and it is **THE** most important period of your dog's whole life. Puppies that miss out tend to be more fearful of all the things they missed out on.

Another disadvantage is that a rescue pup is likely to have been raised in an environment very dissimilar to the average owners' home. Again, we have research to say that pups do much better moving between similar environments than dissimilar i.e. a family household to a family household or an outdoor kennel to an outdoor kennel.

So, What Can Be Done

Well, firstly let us acknowledge there *could* be issues. I am as capable as the next person of burrowing my head in the sand, but when it comes to being the guardian of a new puppy, we need to put our best foot forward.

Firstly, take things much more carefully than perhaps you would with the average pup from a normal breeder, and keep assessing the whole way through. The assessment should be in terms of observation of the pup and how comfortable it looks with the situations you put it in.

Do strangers make the pup particularly uncomfortable?

Does the sound of a barking dog make the pup shake with nervousness?

Do new places have the pup either trying to flee or sitting immobilised?

Is the pup's first reaction to anything new or sudden to be defensive?

Socialisation and Habituation

These are big words for a very important part of your puppy's early learning.

These terms refer to exposure to new things is referred to as Socialisation and Habituation

- In layman terms, socialisation refers to the education that a puppy must receive in order to learn key life skills to ensure that it is confident and comfortable in its world, and can communicate effectively with family members, strangers and other animals.
- Habituation is learning to ignore stimuli that have no consequence. Repeated positive exposure is part of the learning process.

I advise all owners to pay particular attention to these two areas because this is the groundwork for your whole puppy's life! There is no reliving this part. Yes, we can help later. But it is a much better idea to get it right from the start.

I use an acronym to help owners understand this important time and in addition to actually remind them of their role.

SHERPA

A Sherpa is one of the native people who live in the regions of Nepal and the Himalayas. Historically they are elite mountaineers and experts in their local area. Today, everyone knows them as expert guides and mentors to the mountaineers of these extreme peaks and passes, particularly Everest. The term has also become a slang byword for a guide or mentor in other situations.

Owners need to be their pup's Sherpa!

SH – Expose – Reward – Pause – Assess

S ocialisation

H abituation

E xpose the puppy gently to a new experience (sight, sound, smell)

R eward the puppy for calm behaviour via treats, play, praise, strokes and just as importantly moving away from the new experience

P ause to give the pup time to put the memory away – just a few seconds

A ssess – "How is my pup looking; calm, worried, stressed, shaking etc.?" Do I really need to expose my pup again? How shall I expose my pup again? When shall I expose my pup again?

You, as the owner, are the dog trainer. This is your job to be a good trainer and guide.

And remember, food is not generally the best reward a pup can receive. But freedom of choice very often is. The freedom to move away from new and/or scary stuff will always instil confidence and not knock it.

So What Else Should We Consider With Our Pup

I am sometimes pretty stunned by how "good" owners expect their new pup to be when they get it home.

One day it is rolling and wrestling with its littermates, biting, and pouncing, and chewing, and chasing. It sleeps when it likes and has very little worries and few boundaries.

The next it is asked to stop doing all that and is given a lot more space and attention, but suddenly there are boundaries EVERYWHERE!

No wonder it sometimes doesn't all go to plan.

Thank goodness canines are so good at adapting to humans and their wants and needs.

So, let's consider the following to avoid getting upset from the beginning.

THAT OWNER EXPECTATIONS CAN BE TOO HIGH

- No, he will not act straight away like the older dog you already have or have recently lost
- No, he will not understand what it is you want

- No, he is not pushing boundaries
- Yes, your puppy from a decade ago did play bite, chew things, make a mess … You have just forgotten!
- No, maybe your pup will not behave the same as your sister's dog of the same breed
- Yes, maybe you will have to train him to be good around the kids and vice versa, and it will not just happen by magic

Also, we should also consider this too!

THAT OWNERS DON'T REALISE THEY MIGHT NEED TO KNOW MORE

- Owners need to consider how little information they provide to a pup and still expect it to "be good"
- Owners need to understand that a puppy will not know that a behaviour is "wrong"
- Owners need to consider how they may accidentally reward a behaviour
- Owners need to consider how they may accidentally let the environment reward a behaviour

Formal Training

The question is never whether more formal training, such as for recalls and walking nicely, is necessary but simply how are you going to do it!

The more training your pup has the more freedoms he will obtain.

The freedom to run in the park, accompany you into the pub, go on holiday with you, run loose on the beach etc.

Always consider, if you have had a dog previously, what was truly successful and, be honest, what wasn't.

Strike whilst the iron is hot. Start training as soon as the pup is home and even before then make sure you are enrolled on a dedicated puppy training course, preferably one that has been recommended by a friend or family member. Or accost the owner with the best-behaved dog down the park!!!!

The Petrol in Your Pup

There is an awful lot more to creating a fantastic dog.

For one thing, it is well worth thinking about how you fuel your puppy, just as you would a child. There are a lot of poor-quality foods out and that includes the market leaders with flashy advertising and pretty dogs on the packaging.

I once had a behavioural consultation booked for a puppy that was on a current Puppy School course. Now, this is highly unusual as, though pups can be troublesome, pups never normally warrant a full-blown behavioural assessment as early as this in their life. However, this puppy called Molly and was a fourteen-week-old Cockerpoo, and she was driving her owners frantic with her excitability, jumping up and horrid play biting. The husband, in particular, was coming to the end of his tether.

So, they came to see me for their consult on the Saturday, and we included nutrition, of course, as part of the approach.

On the Tuesday, I received this email:

"Well me and Malcolm are just stunned. On the way home on Saturday, we went and bought one of the brands you recommended. And now it as if she has come down off drinking coca-cola! Molly is so much calmer and so more manageable! Yes, still a pup but at least one we can reason with now! Thank you."

So, make sure your pup is fuelled correctly!

Finally

Make sure you have all of the following covered:

- A PLAN! That the whole family understand and are on board with. Same words and same beliefs.
- An understanding that some family members have weaknesses.
- A routine.
- Clear information in every interaction.
- A training programme for essential behaviours and commands.
- A training programme for appropriate socialisation and habituation pre 12 weeks & post 12 weeks.
- Canine enrichment as the norm (An understanding of the breeds needs, and meeting them, is particularly important).
- Exercise in moderation e.g. too much exercise is as bad as too little. Go for quality and not quantity.

This is just a short chapter on how to try and ensure you get the best from your pup. Owners need to remember that the best way to get a GREAT dog is to work really hard on the foundations of the PUP.

Don't build on sand!

Because just around the corner is the adolescent dog! And that is a whole new ball game.

I hope you get on really well with your rescue pup but never be afraid to ask for help, preferably from an expert young dog trainer. Better to get it right at the start of your dog's life.

About the Author

Karen Boyce

Karen Boyce owns Beastly Thoughts Professional Dog Services, one of the biggest dog training organisations in Wales and her home county of Shropshire.

A dog trainer since a child Karen moved officially into instructing owners and dogs in a classroom environment in the '90s and quickly became heavily involved in reactive dog work.

BTPDS was started officially in 2007 and now covers puppies, trained under the Puppy School banner, young and older dogs' general obedience, reactive dogs, Hoopers agility and Rally Obedience. Behavioural consultations are also included in the BTPDS list of services provided.

Karen holds numerous fun events, training workshops, lectures and doggy get-togethers each year. She is a registered trainer with the Animal Behaviour Training Council and is a Kennel Club Rally Judge. She was also awarded the Animal Star Awards Behaviourist of the Year accolade in 2019.

Karen lives on her smallholding in the Llangollen hills overlooking the world-renowned Pontcysyllte Aqueduct, with her daughter Franny and her homebred Elsonway German Shepherds and Elson Shetland Ponies.

www.beastlythoughts.co.uk

Dominic Hodgson

Climbing the Canine Kilimanjaro

I'm going to begin my chapter with a confession, although if you've read any of my other books, then this will come as no great surprise, so here goes.

I'm a very lazy person.

Not only *that*, I'm a proud lazy person too.

If there's an easy way to do anything, then you can bet your butt that I'll be on that idea like a rat on a Cheeto.

And fortunately for you, my desire to keep things as easy as pumpkin pie *also* applies to how I train dogs too.

In *How to Be Your Dog's Superhero,* I identified what I believe are the four keystone needs of a pet dog.

They are;

1. Appropriate exercise
2. Challenge
3. A suitable diet
4. The need to feel safe

Your goal as a new rescue dog owner is to quickly get into the habit of providing activities for your rescue dog that fulfil those four basic needs.

These are going to be your keystone Canine habits, and if you do them daily, you'll find a lot of the initial problems you are experiencing with your rescue dog will not seem so big, and many of them will disappear on their own accord.

I cover the first three basic needs of a dog in my bestselling book How to Be Your Dog's Superhero, so in this chapter, I'm going to focus on the fourth need of a dog, ***the need to feel safe***.

Safety should (in my humble, honest and accurate) opinion be at the forefront of everything you do with your new rescue dog, and to explain a little better we are heading to the African plains...

What's your Kilimanjaro?

In his last year at senior school, my eldest son Alex went on a school trip to Tanzania, where he went on Safari and visited some local schools. The main part of the trip was to climb Mount Kilimanjaro.

I know what you are thinking.

If Chris Moyles can do it for Comic relief how difficult can climbing Kilimanjaro really be? Ok, I'll grant you this there isn't any 'technical climbing' as such, which are moments that have you reaching for an ice axe as you cling onto an overhang. The gradient is quite steady, and you don't even have to carry many kits as there are three local workers to every climber who carry everything they need to make a camp each day.

But climbing Kilimanjaro is way harder than you might think because when you live at sea level as we do, then you will suffer from the main problem that will stop most people reaching the top.

Altitude.

Walking at altitude is a slow game. Imagine an old lady walking backwards, carrying two bags of heavy shopping, and you get the idea of the type of speed you need to travel.

If you were pretty fit, then you could probably get up and down the mountain in just a day, if it wasn't for that darned altitude.

The last part of the climb required the boys to wake up in the early hours of the morning and climb through the night in the hope of reaching the snow-capped summit as the sun rises.

The effects of the altitude were too much for some of the boys, and several were forced to give up due to chronic headaches and nosebleeds.

Our Alex said it was the hardest thing he had ever done, and he had to be almost carried some of the way by his porter.

See despite implementing a rigorous training program and investing in the best equipment and guides to help them to reach the summit, not all the boys made it to the very top.

And whilst reaching the top was the ultimate goal, for me and Beth, Alex simply enjoying the experience and coming home safely was all that mattered to us, and the other parents too, I imagine.

So, safety should come first, always.

If you make keeping yourself, your dog *and* your community safe your number one priority every time step outside your front door, then you will find out that exercising your dog becomes a whole lot easier, and your daily walks will be a lot more enjoyable.

Let's look at each in turn and start with the community.

Why the hell should you care about anyone else? Well, there is an element of society that would like nothing better than to see all dogs on a lead at all times in any public place. Do you want that? Do we want our kids only to see dogs off-lead in dog parks or zoos?

Of course not, but dog's need off-leash exercise and you need to have great control of your dog if you are exercising him off-lead. Remember your dog doesn't need to bite anyone to be considered dangerously out of control, and you then get prosecuted by the law.

Just google Gillian Cobham sues dog owner or Anthony Steele sues for 65K to see how much having an out of control dog can cost you in cold hard cash.

Then there's the dog himself and dog's do stupid things all the time, like running off every time they see a SQUIR-REL!!!! Your dog is very much a 'here and now' type of creature and doesn't think very much in terms of future consequences.

Therefore it's up to YOU to decide what's safe and what isn't, and if your dog wants to do something that will be fun for him but scary, stressful or unsafe for you well then it's your job to put the brakes (or the lead) firmly on.

And let's not forget ourselves in this. I can't be the only one who has felt the gut-wrenching fear in the pit of my stomach that comes when my dog has wandered out of sight for a few minutes and not returned when I called him.

Or said to myself, *'my dog has been really good on this walk I will just let him have five minutes off-leash with this other dog'*. Only for the situation to descend into complete chaos and then the next quarter of an hour is spent trying to get my dog back on lead and apologising to the other dog owners.

So, safety is key, and we are going to make safety a 'key-stone habit' from now on. And it is going to transform your walks with your dog.

The Safety Audit

So, sticking with the audit theme, you are going to ask yourself a very simple question whenever you find yourself in any situation with your rescue dog.

Is this safe?

And then,

How can I make it safer?

Let's add this question to three common everyday scenarios you could find yourself in;

1) Grandma comes for tea every Sunday and Harry the Labrador just loves Grandma. Grandma loves Harry too, and she didn't even blame him when he knocked her over and broke her hip because Harry was just excited, right?

Wrong!

Was it safe?

Of course not.

Everyone knew that Harry gets excited when Grandma comes. So how could you make it safer? By sticking him on lead or removing him from the room for ten minutes until he has calmed down.

2) Ned the Terrier pulls on the lead like a train all the way to the park, and if you are honest, it really hurts. The palms of your hands are sore, your shoulder aches and you will probably end up with RSI in the next year or two (with no one but the dog to sue either!)

So, is it safe?

Well, clearly not if you are in pain.

What happens if he pulls you over and you bust an ankle? You will still love him for sure, but who will walk him? A dog walker will cost money, and a family friend will be unlikely to help once they learn how you busted the ankle.

How can you make it safer? Pre-exhausting the dog by wearing him out before the walk and using a head collar would be the two easiest ways

3) Dusty the Dalmatian is the apple of your eye. You love this dog with all your heart but wish he wasn't so interested in other dogs. He's friendly, and he's playful, and he usually comes back as soon as he has been to say hello, but you always worry about him knocking over a child when he bounds over to greet another family.

So, is it safe?

Absolutely not.

'He's friendly' won't be a suitable excuse in the event of a prosecution if he ends up knocking over a child. And rest assured if it was my child who was injured, I would have no qualms about suing you. I love dogs but have no time for selfish idiots who allow their dogs to do whatever the hell they want.

Please don't think you have too many problems to sort and that you and your dog should probably just close the curtains, lock the door and never leave home again. You can easily apply the safety audit to any situation and ask is it safe? And then if it isn't, then how could you make it safer?

Almost all dog problems can be solved by stopping the dog from doing the thing you don't want him to do and then teaching him something else instead. And stopping him is also going to make life safer and more enjoyable for everyone.

So dear reader, your mission should you choose to accept it, is to identify <u>your Kilimanjaro</u> and then <u>remove the altitude factor</u> so you can make living with your dog much safer.

Here's an example of how I had to put *safety first* with one of my rescue dogs;

Barry was our first Dogue de Bordeaux. We adopted him when he was 18 months old, so we only got some basic knowledge of his life before then from the rescue.

We did know he had been raised in a family and was ok with children. This was a deal-breaker for us with two kids aged 6 and 12 at the time.

Like other Mastiffs, Dobes and GSD's, the DDB was primarily bred as a guarding breed.

This means he is always going to be more likely to display guarding tendencies like a wariness of strangers and a desire to be protective of his property and family.

When you knock on our front door, Barry will let you know in no uncertain terms that he is home and he is big, loud, and you shouldn't come in.

This type of behaviour has its plus points. Everyone knows we have a big, noisy dog and neither us nor our immediate neighbours have ever been burgled (touch wood).

Despite being a belligerent brute through the window once you are invited in, he is a complete pushover. I guarantee he will be lying at your feet for a tummy rub before I've had a chance to offer you a brew.

And if you are the type of person who likes a big, slobbery Dogue, (and why wouldn't you be?), then you will find him rather a handsome dog too.

When I'm out walking civilians will often stop and admire Barry's chops, and they will want to talk to him and even stroke him, and that's where the problem began.

Not long after we got Barry, something happened that caused me concern. I would sometimes stop and chat to people on the way to the park, and they would admire Barry and want to pet him.

This was back when I was a newish dog owner, fairly pleasant and not the anti-social person I am now.

I knew Barry was friendly, as I have described above and so thought he must like meeting people too, but after a few weeks, I noticed that sometimes after the stop and chat, as the person left to go Barry would do a little air bite.

It happened so quick that I didn't see it the first couple of times, then Beth said he had done it with her too, but we remained in denial for a while longer. We wanted Barry to be the perfect dog, and we wanted to be the perfect owners.

No one wants to be the mum and dad to the naughty or aggressive dog, do they?

So rather than do anything about it, I would make excuses for him.

And owners of rescue dogs are generally the world's worst for making excuses for their dog's behaviour. *'Sorry, he's a rescue' 'He's just afraid because he's a rescue' 'He doesn't like other dogs, people, big dogs, small dogs, buses, policemen* because he's a rescue....'*

*insert your dog's thing here.

I know *why* rescue dog owners do this, it's because we feel bad about our dogs past and we think it's not the dog's fault they act a certain way. To a degree that's true, but there's a fine line between being forgiving of mistakes your dog makes and sticking your head in the sand about a problem behaviour that needs fixing.

And I was definitely sticking my head in the sand about Barry's air-biting.

One day he did it again and managed to grab a tissue out of my neighbour's hand as he turned to walk away from me. As people do the guy was apologising for Barry, but I finally realised this was a pretty serious problem and needed sorting.

What if next time it wasn't the tissue but the skin?

So, after chatting with Beth, we decided unless they were family or close friends then no one would be allowed to touch Barry at all.

And after that, life got much easier for us all. Now we know what we were going to do in every situation. It wasn't a case of does this person look friendly or has Barry seen this person before. No one was allowed to touch him.

In short, I asked: Is it safe? And then how can I make it safer?

If I met someone who wanted to talk to me, then I would position Barry behind me, ask him to sit, and *then* chat.

If the person asked could they stroke him, I would say *'No, he is friendly, but he doesn't like strangers.'* There were no exceptions <u>ever.</u>

Once I got into the habit things got much easier, very quickly.

It must have been a tremendous relief for Barry as well, now all he had to worry about was walking beside me.

I eventually realised I had to be cruel to be kind just to keep our Bordeaux happy when we took him to the park.

You might have to make a similar decision with your rescue dog.

If you think your dog will make the wrong choice (and do something that's potentially dangerous) then taking the decision making out of your dog's hands is the sensible thing to do.

Remember you're his owner, that's what you are *supposed* to do.

Once I'd made that decision, it meant Barry didn't have to worry about anyone touching him.

By putting safety first, I removed the need for him to ask himself, *'Do I have to defend my mam or say hello to this person?'* every time we met someone at the park.

Now he just has to sit and wait while I talked. I made sure of diffusing the flashpoint of when the person walked away by just telling Barry to sit again and then shoving a treat under his nose, which I gave him as we walked away.

Yes, we had to piss a few people off, but truthfully, I don't care about that.

Sometimes I think I probably annoyed Barry as well, as he may have thought this person looks really nice, I want to say hello.

Tough shit I'm afraid Barry.

My priority is making him feel safe, and me keeping everyone else safe in my community.

What it uncomfortable at times?

Yes

Is it necessary?

Absolutely it is!

So, what can you learn from this?

Well as harsh as this might sound, you dear reader are the person most qualified to make decisions on behalf of your rescue dog.

Not the person you meet in the park. (as well-meaning as they might be)

And *not* your dog either (Dogs are pretty selfish, remember and will always think about what they want, which often isn't the safest or most appropriate thing to do)

So, you decide what's best to keep your dog safe, and *then* stick to it.

Trust me on this.

Your dog, if he could, would thank you for it.

About the Author

Dominic Hodgson

Dom Hodgson's plain speaking, no B.S, forthright views about dog training have earned him the moniker, *The King of Canine Common Sense*. Dom is passionate about helping dogs and owners enjoy fantastic relationships together, and he believes kind, effective, common-sense dog training is the way to ensure more dogs stay with their owners and stay out of shelters.

You can grab any of Dom's eight books from Amazon, or you can get the free ebook version of *How to Be Your Dog's Superhero* by visiting tourderescue.com

Conclusion

Taking on a rescue dog is incredibly rewarding, in many cases you are literally saving a life, but let's not kid ourselves, it can also be bloody hard work.

When he's first removed from his home and put in a rescue, the dog is separated from everything he's ever known.

He's placed in a strange and scary environment where everything is new to him (including his bed, food, routine, the carers and any canine company he temporarily lives with).

Usually, the dog is being rehomed because he's been abused or his behaviour is such that his original owner can't control him. With all that going on, it's no wonder that rescuing a dog is so stressful.

To make the transition as easy as possible, you need a lot of patience, *and* a plan to follow. A plan that put the dog first, and helps him to adapt to his new routine in what will hopefully be his forever home.

It can take a rescue dog a few weeks to a few months for him to truly 'settle in'. Certainly, you won't see his real self until he thoroughly checked out the lie of the land and feels comfortable. Of course, this depends on how long he spent in rescue and what behavioural problems he developed during or before he was placed in a shelter.

As you read in the previous chapter, my Dogue de Bordeaux Barry's guarding traits didn't show themselves until he's been with us for a few months. He'd spent a couple of weeks in a shelter before we got him and was visibly traumatised by the experience, very cautious, nervous and unsure of himself for the first week or so in our home.

Compare that with Derek the Bordeaux who we adopted in 2017 through Dogue de Bordeaux Rescue and Rehoming UK. Derek was an eight month old delinquent whose original owner was struggled to manage so was looking for a new home for him. I was fortunate enough to be able to drive and collect Derek from his home, so he never experienced being in a shelter, and the transition to his new home with us was much less stressful. Although Beth and I sometimes joke maybe it would have been good for him to have spent a night or two on his own in a shelter, just to make him appreciate how good his life is now with us! Yep, even Dom spoils his dogs now and again.

Our first dog Flo was around nine weeks when we got her in 1998. With hindsight it's obvious to see she'd been taken from her mother too soon, and was lacking a lot of basic socialisation (which I made worse by not taking the advice of our vet and didn't take her outside for another three weeks)

The point I'm making here is every rescue dog is going to come with his own unique set of personal issues, and some are going to be potentially more problematic than others.

However, as you've seen from the inspiring stories in this book, *most* problems can be overcome. If you feel lost and don't know how to move forward with your rescue dog, then please contact a professional trainer who has hands-on experience in helping rescue dogs.

With patience, a plan and some professional help to guide you, you'll soon make progress with your own rescue dog.

This has been a really fun book to put together. Since the inception of the Tour de Rescue I've come into contact with so many amazing dog trainers, charities, rescue volunteers, and of course, the rescue dogs themselves, and it's fitting we have created what I think will be an important resource that helps rescue dog owners adapt to their new addition.

Please help me to help more dogs and owners stay together, and get more dogs out of shelters by sharing this book, and the ideas in it with any rescue dog owners and friends you have who are thinking about adopting a rescue dog.

Acknowledgements

I would like to offer my sincere thanks to all my friends and colleagues who contributed to this book, which I hope will be a great help to anyone who has a rescue, or is just thinking about getting one.

So, from the bottom of my walking boots, I'd like to 'BIG UP' the dog trainers and writers Katie Guastapaglia, Dan Alberts, Carol Clark, Tim Jackson, Suzanne Gould, Steven Wylie, Adam Delderfield, Emma Lee, Sarah Bartlett and Karen Boyce.

Please check out these guys' books and services. They're all truly awesome!

Huge thanks to my wife and operations manager at Pack Towers, Beth for putting this book together.

Also David and the team at Writermotive.com for sorting the formatting and cover.

My good mate Bill Goss at Elite Publishing for his continued help and support.

And also to my own dogs Derek, Sidney, Barry and the rescue runt whose arrival inadvertently changed my life, little Flo.

I'd also like to give a huge shout out to all of the rescue centres I visited during the Tour de Rescue event, please check out *and* support these amazing organisations, or your local animal rescue centre.

Bryson's Animal Shelter , Gateshead - www.brysons.org.uk

SHAK Sanctuary , Alnwick - www.shak.org.uk

Alexa's Animals , Alnwick - www.alexasanimals.com

Hope Animal Shelter , Loftus – www.hopeanimalshelter.co.uk

Maxies Mates , Teeside – www.maxiesmates.org.uk

Save Our Strays , Redcar – www.saveoustrays.org.uk

Heart Welfare (Husky) – www.heartwelfare.co.uk

The Edward Foundation (Bulldog) – www.theedwardfoundation.co.uk

Crowfoot Animal Rescue , Derbyshire – www.crowfootkennels.co.uk

Ashbourne Animal Welfare , Ashbourne - www.ashbourneanimalwelfare.org

Just for Dogs , Ashbourne – www.justfordogs.co.uk

Moorlands Dog Rescue , Leek – www.moorlandsrescue.com

Ark Angels Rescue , Chester – Find on Facebook

Almost Home Dog Rescue , Mold – www.almosthomedogrescue.dog

Hectors Greyhound Rescue (greyhound) - www.hectorsgreyhoundrescue.org

You can find out more about the Tour de Rescue and download a FREE copy of my bestselling book *How to Be Your Dog's Superhero* by going to www.tourderescue.com

Finally, thanks to you dear reader for investing in and reading this book.

Please do me a massive favour and leave a nice review on Amazon, and share what you learned with your rescue dog owning pals.

Let's make rescue dogs the default option for dog owners.

Take care, and once again, don't forget to support your local rescue!

Your pal

Dom Hodgson
www.mydogssuperhero.com
www.growyourpetbusinessfast.com

About the Author

Dom Hodgson is a dog adventurer, 'superhero' dog trainer, rescue dog advocate, and the UK's most respected, sought after and controversial pet business coach.

In 2011 Dom launched his first business 'Pack Leader Dog Adventures' which revolutionised the dog walking industry by transforming the usual dog walking services from a 'boring toilet walk around the block' to a training adventure experience that helps busy dog owners with stay at home dogs, enjoy a full, active and stress-free life.

In 2016 Dom wrote the Amazon bestselling *'How to Be Your Dog's Superhero'* which for the first time delivered a 'real-life' dog training blueprint that any pet dog owner can use to have more control and more fun with their dogs.

In 2019 Dom founded the Tour de Rescue event. This is a fund (and awareness) raising event to highlight great work done by small local rescue centre volunteers who work on the front line in their canine community.

Dom is a much in-demand speaker and his dog training seminars and pet business bootcamps in which he delivers the same No BS, jargon-free advice he dispenses in his unique writing style which has won him thousands dog and human admirers, all over the world.

Dom hosts two 'hit' podcast shows **'Dom Hodgson's Dogcast'** and **'The Poodle to Pitbull Pet Business Podcast'**, download and listen wherever you get your pods.

He lives on in an old farmhouse in Sunderland in the North East of England, with his wife Beth, sons Alex and

Toby, dogs, Derek the Dogue de Bordeaux and Sid the Cocker, and eight chickens. When not working Dom can usually be found walking his dogs on the beach.

Other Books by the Author

Dog Training Books

How to Be Your Dog's Superhero: Transform your dastardly dog into a perfect pooch in just six weeks

Worry Free Walks: How to transform your dangerous, difficult and devilish dog into a problem-free pooch that you're proud to take to the park

The Perfect Puppy Project: The ultimate no-mess, zero-stress, step-by-step guide to raising the perfect puppy

The Lazy Dog Owners Ten Minute Training Plan: The quick, easy and no B.S guide to turn your dastardly dog into a perfect pooch

The Dog Owners Self-Isolation Survival Guide: Discover how to quickly and easily exercise, entertain and emotionally connect with your dog from the seclusion of your sitting room

Pet Business Books

Walk Yourself Wealthy: The quick, easy and no BS guide to transform your passion for pooches into an insanely profitable and fun dog walking empire

The Ultimate Pet Business Plan: How to launch, grow and scale an outrageously profitable, impactful and fun pet business that dominates your local town

Printed in Great Britain
by Amazon

24964385R00090